Designing Computer-Based
Learning Materials

Designing Computer-Based Learning Materials

Alan Clarke

Gower

Published by
Gower Publishing Limited
Gower House
Croft Road
Aldershot
Hampshire GU11 3HR
England

Gower Publishing Company
131 Main Street
Burlington VT 05401-5600 USA

Alan Clarke has asserted his right under the Copyright, Designs and Patents Act 1988 to be identified as the author of this work.

British Library Cataloguing in Publication Data

Clarke, Alan
    Designing computer-based learning materials
    1. Computer-assisted instruction – Authoring programs
    I. Title
    371.3'34

ISBN 0 566 08320 5

Library of Congress Cataloging-in-Publication Data

Clarke, Alan, 1952–
    Designing computer-based learning materials / Alan Clarke.
        p. cm.
    Includes index.
    ISBN 0-566-08320-5 (hard)
        1. Computer-assisted instruction--Authoring programs. 2. Instructional systems--Design. 3. Learning. I. Title.

    LB1028.66.C53 2001
    371.33'4--dc21   2001033402

Typeset in 11pt Times by IML Typographers, Birkenhead and printed in Great Britain by TJ International, Padstow.

Contents

List of figures

List of tables

Introduction

Designing computer-based learning materials is a complex task involving a mix of factors and variables. It is not a straightforward matter of following a recipe to achieve the perfect outcome. It involves careful consideration of many issues not least the context in which the materials will be used, the individual learners and the objectives of the product. Good practice is frequently context related so that simply transferring a design from one context to another is no guarantee of success. The designer runs the real risk of failure.

This book attempts to reveal the many complex and related issues involved in designing computer-based learning. It discusses the different factors in order to provide you with an understanding of the issues which influence the design of effective learning materials. A range of tools is available to help the designer to create learning materials. However, they do no guarantee that the structure, content, learning design or fresh ideas that will be needed will achieve your aims. They simply make it easy to transfer your design to the screen. This book is tool free in that it is about learning design not software production.

This is not a 'How to ...' book but rather one seeking to help you understand the different elements which go into computer-based learning. It will help if you are commissioning materials to understand the contractor's constraints. It will allow you to avoid many of the errors it is too easy to make when developing and designing materials. You need to consider the ideas presented and transfer them to your situation. Many of the examples are generic in order to provide you with ideas free of too much obstruction.

Chapter 1

Interaction and learning

By the end of this chapter you will have been introduced to:

- the features of computer-based learning
- characteristics of the learners
- the relationship between interaction and learning
- the different degrees of interaction
- the role that questions and feedback can play in interaction
- how navigation can enhance interaction
- human-to-human interaction.

Computer-based learning

Computer-based learning has the potential to provide a highly motivating learning experience through the use of engaging and adaptable material. However, to fulfil this potential requires the exploitation of those features which it offers for the delivery and support of learning.

The main features are:

- presentation and combination of multiple media (for example, graphics/still images, sound, animation, video, colour and text)
- adaptability (for example, able to change to suit the learners' needs, style and pace)
- dynamic display (for example, windows, scrolling and hypertext links)
- memory (for example, record learners' reactions, test results and pattern of learning)
- patience (for example, computers make no judgement if learners need many attempts to understand the content)
- tirelessness (for example, never need to take a break or go on holiday)

- interactivity (for example, able to respond to the learners' reactions, behaviour and choices).

The critical feature of computer-based learning which makes it different from other media is interactivity – that is, the power of the computer to engage, communicate and adapt to the learner. Learning is an active process, so simply presenting information on a screen is unlikely to be successful. Learners must be able to interact with the content by making choices and receiving feedback. If learners get a question wrong the computer-based learning package can offer feedback to help them to understand why their answer was incorrect. The material can be designed to test their preferred learning style and then alter the presentation and sequence to best meet the learners' preference. In a similar way they can be tested for their knowledge of the subject so that they are not asked to study material they already understand. In addition many choices can be offered to the learners so that they can personally customize the learning experience.

Characteristics of the learners

Interaction depends on the stimuli that the computer-based learning material can present to the learners. Different learners will respond to stimuli in a range of ways so it is important to be aware of the characteristics of the group you are designing for. The factors which may influence the learners' response include:

- age
- computer literacy
- previous experience of computer-based learning
- educational experience
- learning skills
- gender
- physical characteristics
- reading age
- knowledge of the subject
- first language.

These factors will be considered in more detail in later chapters but the design of computer-based learning should always commence with a consideration of the learners' needs and characteristics. For example:

1. Learners who have never used a computer could find interacting with a display by pointing and clicking with a mouse so distracting that they ignore the learning material in favour of the challenge the mouse presents.
2. Men are more likely to be colour blind than women so material which relies solely on an object changing colour to provide feedback may not be perceived by a proportion of male users.
3. Older learners may not have the manual dexterity to operate input devices with the degree of accuracy required.

In addition to looking at learner needs and characteristics, the designer should consider what are the features of successful learning and how computer-based learning can provide them.

Adult learning

Materials and activities which support successful adult learning must:

- be relevant and meaningful to the learners
- allow for the extensive life experience of adults
- allow for the different motives of the learners
- engage all the learners' senses
- allow for the different learning styles of the learners.

Interactive computer-based learning materials have the potential to provide these features since they:

- use a range of media to engage all the senses and motivate the learners
- can be designed to provide individualized experiences
- can be designed to adapt to the different learning styles of the learners
- provide learning in meaningful chunks
- can allow material and media to be selected to meet learners' needs and characteristics
- maximize learners' choices to enable them to select what is appropriate to meet their own needs
- provide opportunities for self-assessment.

However, in all cases to realize the potential of computer-based learning requires effective interactive design.

What is interaction?

Good tutors will adapt their methods to the learners' needs and behaviour. They will observe the learners and change their approach according to the reaction of the students. If they are finding a subject difficult the tutors should present it in a different way (for example, by using more examples). Equally, they can speed up their delivery if the group are finding it too easy. The tutor and student are communicating with each other and both will make changes to suit the other. In a similar way, computer-based learning material and the learner must take part in a two-way dialogue. Each must change and adapt to the other.

Figure 1.1 shows the process between the material and the learners that takes place through the computer interface. The interface is important in that it presents the stimuli to which the learners react as well as providing feedback to them about their response to the stimuli.

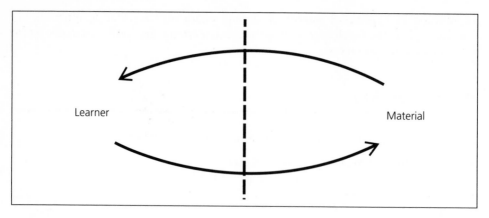

Figure 1.1   Simple interaction

Successful learning depends on a high degree of interaction between the learners and the material. Interaction is not simply about making the learners touch the keys or click on icons. It is about engaging their minds. Learners must be motivated, engaged and excited by computer-based learning. They must be able to:

- consider options
- sort information
- draw conclusions
- answer questions
- take notes
- reach decisions
- take action
- reflect on what they are experiencing
- make inferences.

Computer-based learning has the potential to provide extensive interaction and therefore be a powerful means of delivering learning experiences. Nevertheless it is perfectly possible to produce some computer-based learning which is almost free of interaction. Described as electronic page turning, it is little more than a book presented on the screen. The degree of interaction and engagement in simply clicking on a button to turn the page is likely to be minimal. The learners' choice is limited to moving forward and back. Yet this is preferable to forcing the learner to watch passively a sequence of displays without any option to interrupt their flow or stop the action. Short sequences of page turning can be acceptable.

Interactivity implies making purposeful links and not random selections. The learners make deliberate selections about where to go next and what to do. They are engaged in learning about the subject, not wandering aimlessly from screen to screen (for example, like flicking through television channels with a remote control). The learners have a purpose which they are trying to achieve through interacting with the contents of the computer-based learning.

Many people would consider that a learner reading a book is a passive process. However, if you observe readers with an objective they are very active. They do not simply read from the first to the last page. They make conscious decisions about what to read. They browse the contents, read selected items, consider the index and table of contents, place bookmarks at locations that they identify as important and make notes. This is an active process in which the reader is interacting with the book. The book's content is motivating the reader. In a similar way computer-based learning needs to stimulate the learners to pursue their aims. The computer provides far more potential for interaction and presentation of content than a book.

Interaction is about:

- active participation and engagement
- learning by doing
- making decisions
- selecting between options
- providing individualized feedback
- alternative choices
- motivation.

Interaction is not about:

- passive viewing of material
- absorbing information like a sponge
- allowing the system to make your decisions
- single routes through the material.

Degrees of interaction

The degree of interaction depends on:

- presenting the contents in a motivating and engaging way
- providing effective feedback on the learners' performance
- maximizing the choices available to the learners
- providing activities to enhance learning, such as tests and questions.

This chapter will introduce you to all four of these elements in order to build on their roles later in the book.

The degree of interaction in computer-based learning material will vary considerably between and within packages. The levels of interaction below place an emphasis on learners' choice and navigation. This is a simplification of interaction and the factors of engagement, motivation and adaptability that were discussed earlier must also be considered.

Four levels of interaction are:

1. Foundation level: A television programme is a linear presentation of content which learners can only stop and start. They have little control over the

programme. However, the content of the presentation can be interesting and motivating but is essentially passive. Learning is an active process.

2. Basic level: An information terminal in a railway station presents the users with a limited range of options from which they can select. Learners can choose between the options and observe the information their selection provides for them. This basic level of interaction provides users with not only the ability to stop and start the display but also a limited degree of choice. This may be sufficient if your learners are already highly motivated but it does little to provide them with the motivation to study its content.

3. Intermediate level: A modern operating system (for example, Microsoft Windows) provides the users with many alternative ways of achieving an objective – choices of route, clear feedback and a consistent approach. Learners can explore their environment with feedback to assist their decisions, observe, read and view illustrations, answer questions, reflect on material and select from options while the system reacts to their responses. This type of system provides a rich environment in terms of choice but it must be integrated with the content to also provide a stimulating learning experience.

4. Advanced level: An aircraft simulator provides a lifelike experience of flying a plane whereby trainee pilots can practise the many skills and procedures in which they need to become competent. Learning by doing is the main method with choices and feedback similar to those available in the real situation. The learners are free to try in perfect safety, approaches which would be dangerous, impracticable or expensive. Advanced level interaction attempts to provide lifelike experiences with the same degree of choice, feedback and freedom.

Foundation

A foundation level of interaction could be designed as a tutorial on key events during the American Civil War (see Figure 1.2). In this package the learners are presented with three buttons from which they can choose. If the learners click on any button then a screen is displayed showing a list of battles and dates. After a set interval, the system returns to the initial display.

The interaction is limited, with the learners merely being able to start a process (that is, display a list of battles). If this were the total content of the material it is doubtful whether the learners would be very motivated or engaged by the presentation. However, if it was combined with other media or part of a larger package, then it could be acceptable. If the display was accompanied by a sound commentary describing that year of the war in terms of the battles displayed, it could be substantially improved.

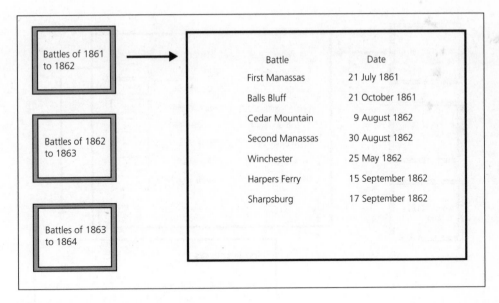

Figure 1.2   Foundation interaction

Basic

The foundation level of interaction could easily be improved by the addition of some extra options allowing the learners to select appropriate choices. Figure 1.3 shows some of these extra features. They are:

- an optional sound commentary
- an option to learn more about each battle (for example, More)
- a go back one page button (for example, Back)
- a jump button to return to the opening display (for example, Return).

This type of interaction is often seen in computer-based learning material and by relatively simple additions offers far more choice to the learners than the foundation example. The degree of interaction has been significantly enhanced, though it is still limited.

It relies on the motivation the learners bring with them to the package. Adults are often self-motivated but this type of computer-based learning is probably best suited to simple browsing through the material rather than concentrated and focused study. Browsing is an effective approach when combined with other methods.

Intermediate

The next step increases the degree of interaction by adding more options and

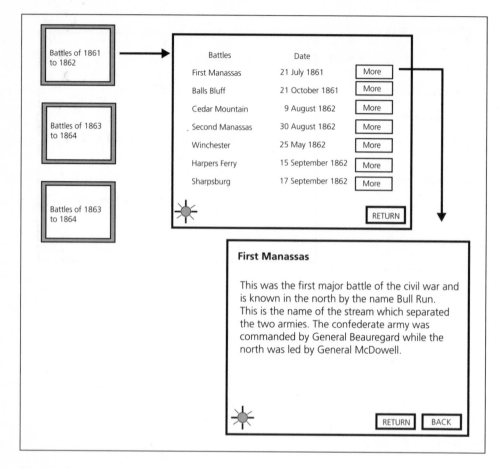

Figure 1.3   Basic interaction

choices of media and by providing feedback (see Figure 1.4). In this version of our tutorial the learners are provided with:

- an optional sound commentary of each specific battle complete with a small library of still images of the battle
- access to a quiz about the battle (a number of questions are presented randomly so learners cannot predict what they will be asked)
- feedback after their response to the question
- an extra feedback option to learn more about the particular topic
- a note taking facility. By clicking on the Notes button learners can enter notes into a simple word-processor. The file created can be printed or transferred at the end of the tutorial. The learners are encouraged by this facility to consider what they are experiencing and summarize their views as a set of notes.

The learners are offered a considerable degree of choice alongside assessment,

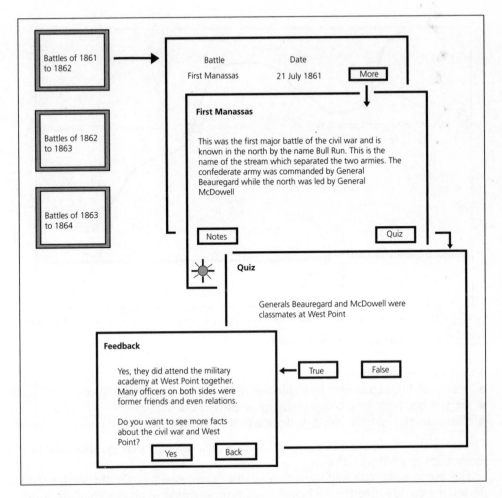

Figure 1.4   Intermediate interaction

complete with feedback. The degree of interaction and opportunities for learning have been significantly increased.

Advanced

An advanced interaction provides learners with an environment which simulates real-life experiences. Learners are able to explore the environment, try out different approaches and experience the results. Figure 1.5 shows a simulation of the Battle of First Manassas. It allows the learners to:

● act the part of both commanders and gain the viewpoint of both armies
● play against the computer or another learner

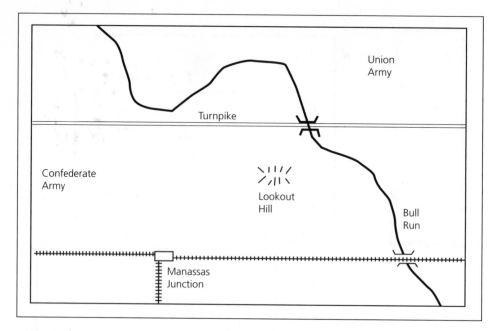

Figure 1.5   Manassas battle microworld

- explore the environment
- gain real-life experience by exploring options and witnessing results
- experience how long actions take to be carried out
- carry out the historic battle or decide to try out their own tactics.

The simulation is operated by a set of rules which are intended to reflect the real restrictions of civil war armies.

The complexity and sophistication of the microworld is for the designer to decide but could range from a board game type situation to an environment using video of the actual battlefield, sound effects and built-in tutorials to explain the choices the historical generals made. In both cases the learners have many opportunities to explore ideas, experiment with different tactics and solutions and experience the decisions which needed to be made. This is a high degree of interaction compared to simply turning electronic pages.

Simulations and microworlds have been developed for many different situations such as:

- flight simulators
- manufacturing goods
- health and safety – hazard spotting
- controlling crowds
- fighting fires
- managing resources
- exploring historical incidents.

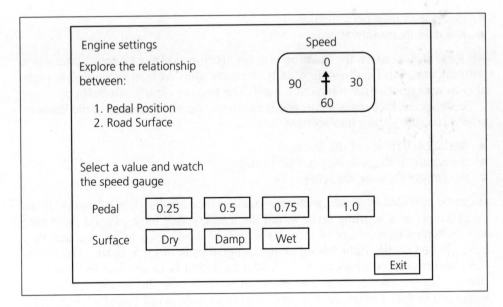

Figure 1.6   **Engine simulation**

Although developing a flight simulator is a complex and expensive undertaking, a simulation/microworld can be incorporated into many situations without vast expenditure. Figure 1.6 provides an example of a small simulation. Essentially it is a microworld for investigating acceleration and road surfaces. The students are asked to experiment with four setting of the accelerator pedal and three different road surfaces to observe the effects on the speed of a car.

Mixed

A mixed level uses a number of different degrees of interaction and provides a variety of approaches, which helps to maintain the learners' interest. The engine simulation could be linked to a series of electronic books providing detailed information on different aspects of engines, rather like workshop manuals. This mixed approach is probably the most commonly used in computer-based learning.

Feedback

All levels of interaction are enhanced by the provision of feedback. Feedback can help the learners:

● make informed choices
● engage with the learning material

- assess their own performance
- maintain their motivation.

All these factors assist the learning process and increase the learners' interaction with the material. Feedback is usually provided after an interaction and is probably as important as the interaction itself. The two are clearly interrelated.

Feedback can take many forms and is more than simply correction of the learners' errors. It needs to take into account:

- the characteristics of the learners
- the nature of the task they are performing
- the subject they are studying.

It can be provided as words, pictures, sound or as a combination of media. It can be as simple as a warning noise to tell the learners they have pressed the wrong key, button or icon. Users of all software applications need to be sure that they have clicked on the right button or the temptation is to click again, which may have unfortunate consequences. A standard solution is to animate the button so that it changes shape when you click on it. This straightforward feedback is important in that it helps the learners recover from or avoid mistakes. Figure 1.7 illustrates the before and after states of a button which has been clicked. The users can clearly see they have been successful.

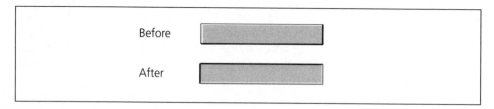

Figure 1.7   Animated buttons

More complex feedback frequently follows questions or other forms of assessment. Some examples of feedback are:

- marks and grades
- comments on strengths and weaknesses
- model answers
- hints and tips to improve performance
- worked examples.

Simply telling learners that they have given a wrong answer is unlikely to engage them. Better feedback would be to explain why the answer is wrong. Effective feedback:

- is positive
- is immediate
- corrects learners' responses

- explains why the response is right or wrong
- provides assistance
- links to earlier responses.

Questions

Feedback often follows a response to a question. By asking questions you are both assessing learners' understanding and helping them to interact with the learning material. It is important to recognize that each level of interaction can be improved by incorporating questions into the design of the material. There are many different ways of presenting questions and Chapter 4 will cover these in some detail. The learners' response to a question can be used to determine what feedback they need and help the system determine the route they should follow through the rest of the material. For example:

- a series of wrong answers may indicate the need to route the individual through a section to review the material again or to present remedial exercises
- a series of right answers may show the need to start presenting the learner with more advanced or difficult content.

This changing of routes is often called branching and Figure 1.8 shows an example of branching in the form of a flow chart. The figure is simplified and would normally show feedback for all types of answer and the opportunity to have more than one attempt at each question. It does reveal that it is possible to use an assessment in the form of a question to branch learners into different types of material.

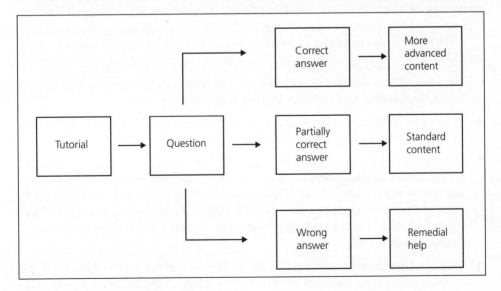

Figure 1.8   **Branching flow chart**

There are two distinct approaches to branching:

1. Assessment tests can be included in the material to allow the system to determine the route the learner takes and the degree of difficulty of the content. However, many learners will deliberately get a question wrong in order to discover what happens, so it is often good practice not to score these questions as part of the overall assessment unless you clearly tell the learners that is your intention.

2. The learner can be allowed to make the choice.

The best approach is to combine both. In our flow chart example learners could be given advice to select the more advanced material but they are free to opt for the remedial help instead. This works provided you are sure they have sufficient understanding of the topic to make an effective choice. If you are in doubt then make the selection automatic. In many cases the learners are unaware that the system has branched unless you inform them.

Navigation

Navigation is a key element in the design of computer-based learning material. It has a considerable influence on interactivity. When learners read a textbook they are provided with a range of navigation aids such as a contents list, an index, lists of figures and page numbers. These devices are not easy to transfer from the textbook because computer-based learning employs a variety of media. Research has often suggested that learners find it difficult to visualize computer-based material and often report feelings of being lost. Learning is unlikely to be enhanced if learners are unsure of where they are, doubtful of how to return to earlier material and suspicious of which choice to make because they don't know where it will take them.

A number of navigational mechanisms are available to the designer. These include:

- Forward and back buttons – individuals can retrace their steps in a similar way that a book reader can refer backwards and forwards.

- A bar which fills up as the learners work through the module. This provides a visual indication of how much is left to study.

- Main menu/home page – this is often the first display the learners encounter and is essentially the contents page. It allows them to jump directly to each section of the material. In turn, each frame of the material is linked directly back to the main menu or home page. Figure 1.9 provides an example of this approach. Websites are normally organized around a home page to aid users' navigation of the site.

- Map – an overview map is provided at the start of the material to allow the learners to gain an understanding of the structure of the material. Figure 1.10 provides an example of a map of a computer-based learning tutorial.

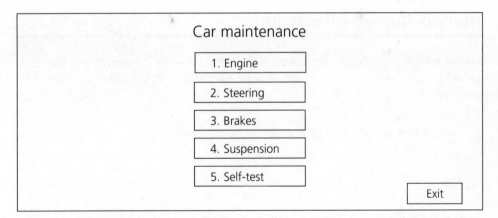

Figure 1.9   **Main menu**

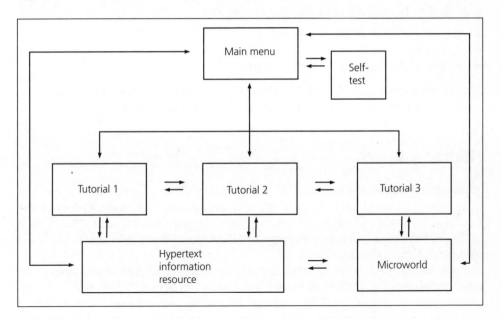

Figure 1.10   **Map showing structure of computer-based learning material**

- Search engine – the means of searching for a particular topic throughout the whole contents and is perhaps best described as an electronic index.

- Page numbers, for example, 12 of 45 – this tells users where they are in the module and how much is left. However, a design which is based on a fixed linear route of 45 pages is unlikely to engage learners or use the medium to its best effect.

Human–human interaction

So far we have assumed that interaction is between the computer and the individual learner. However, there are at least two other situations which should be considered:

1. interaction supplied by a tutor
2. interaction when a pair of learners work together.

Tutor

CBL can be used as a group resource by projecting the material on to a large screen. The interaction is controlled by the tutor who can stop and start the display. The tutor can add to the interactivity by:

- asking questions of the whole group
- setting extra activities
- generally building on the CBL resources.

This is not a common use of CBL material but it can be a powerful aid to learning by combining good face-to-face instruction with the best in CBL.

Pairs of learners

Although CBL is often discussed in the context of one person working on their own there is a considerable body of research and practical evidence that value can be added by a pair of learners interacting with the material and each other. This is almost always based on schoolchildren but there is no reason why adults could not also benefit from this approach.

Each learner has the extra advantage of the other. The partner can help overcome problems. The human-to-human discussion can help develop understanding, extend the contents of the CBL material by adding the individual experience of two learners and provide two viewpoints on the subject. However, balancing these benefits, there is the danger that one learner controls the CBL so that the other is denied any choice over the material considered.

Retention

All forms of open and distance learning including computer-based learning can suffer from very high rates of learners failing to complete the course. It is fairly normal in excellent learning environments with considerable personal support such as mentors and coaches to have a 20 per cent failure rate. Without good support the rates can easily exceed 50 per cent. There are many different approaches to providing support but most people involved have a role to play.

The learning centre receptionist can help with using the equipment, locating the right packages and providing a friendly service. Peer support can help maintain motivation and often allows learners to ask each other questions which they believe are too simple to ask a tutor. Successful learners who have already completed the course or are knowledgeable about the subject can often act as mentors to current learners. A mentor is anyone who has experience of studying using computer-based learning or of the contents or both. They will understand how the learner is feeling and what are the most difficult parts of the subject. They can advise the learner when things get difficult or simply listen to them. A mentor is often a role model whom the learner can try to emulate. Mentors are usually colleagues, peers or managers.

Online learning is rapidly growing with the learners accessing the material from a wide range of locations including their own workplace, libraries, learning centres and their homes. This makes providing face-to-face support more difficult but does open up the possibilities of remote support using e-mail, electronic conferencing and mailgroups. Online support is effectively available continuously. However, it is still relatively early days for online support and most organizations are still experimenting with different approaches. E-mail is an excellent communication medium for answering questions or for short discussions but it is not easy for a mentor to diagnose problems or to realize a learner needs someone to talk to. Electronic conferencing and mailgroups can provide excellent access to other learners and hence to peer support but both suffer from very low participation rates.

Summary of key points

Computer-based learning

- Interactivity is a critical feature of computer-based learning which makes it different from other media.

Characteristics of the learners

- Learners respond to stimuli depending on their individual characteristics.

Adult learning

- Computer-based learning must actively involve learners.
- Learners communicate with the learning materials through the computer interface. This is called interaction.

- Interactive computer-based learning materials have the potential to provide effective learning experiences which motivate, adapt to individual differences, meet learners' needs, maximize choice and allow for self-assessment.

Degrees of interaction

The degree of interaction varies and four levels can be defined. These are described in Table 1.1.

Table 1.1   *Degrees of interaction*

Degree of interaction	Description
Foundation	Interaction limited to starting the process
Basic	Users can start and stop interaction and also make some limited choices
Intermediate	Users have significant choice of route through material as well as being able to start, go back, return and stop the presentation. The system also provides extensive feedback to the learners
Advanced	Continuous interaction and feedback as learners explore the environment. They have considerable freedom of choice

- Foundation level is essentially a linear presentation of material.
- Basic level adds more choice to the foundation level so that learners can choose between a number of options.
- Intermediate level involves significantly more learner choice and control combined with feedback.
- Advanced level interaction provides learners with the opportunity to explore and experiment with an environment similar to a real-life situation.
- Many CBL packages combine different degrees of interaction.

Feedback

- As an aid to learning, feedback is as important as interaction.
- Feedback is not simply a matter of informing learners that they are right or wrong. It can relate to a single interaction or a series of interactions.
- Feedback needs to reflect the characteristics of the learner (for example, age, gender, experience and so on), the subject being studied and the environment where learning is taking place.

Questions

- Questions are useful in generating interaction but also serve to determine whether the learners need extra help to understand the material.
- Branching of CBL material can be controlled by the computer, the learners or a mixture of the two.

Navigation

- CBL needs navigation devices like those provided in a book to assist learners in finding their way around the material and avoid the danger of feeling lost.
- CBL needs navigation aids such as page numbering (for example, 12 from 45), forward and back buttons, main menu or home pages, structural maps and search engines.

Human–human interaction

Interaction is not limited to an individual learner working with CBL material but also includes:

- teacher and group interactions
- pairs of learners interacting with CBL and each other.

Retention

- Support is vital to the successful completion of computer-based learning.

Chapter 2

Communication styles

By the end of this chapter you will have been introduced to:

- a comparison of CBL and traditional learning methods
- communication aids
- interaction of learner, subject and environment
- a range of communication styles including commands, menus, question and answers, form fill, direct manipulation and natural language
- the use of metaphor in design.

Communication aids within computer-based learning materials

It is very easy to get so carried away by the exciting nature of computer-based learning that you forget some of the fundamentals. A critical factor is to inform learners about the nature of the learning experience that they are going to engage in. This involves several different forms of communication. The first is likely to be explaining to learners the objectives of the learning experience. Objectives can be gaining additional knowledge (for example, understanding a new procedure) or skills (for example, knowing how to operate a piece of machinery) or in changes of attitudes brought about by the package (for example, customer relations).This is normally expressed in terms of what they will be able to do after studying the materials.

Example
After studying the materials you will be able to:

1. understand the nature of . . .
. 2. discuss . . .

3.   select which is the most effective . . .
4.   repair . . .

After studying the module you will understand:

1.   how to . . .
2.   when to . . .
3.   where . . .

Learners can identify with this type of description since it tells them what they can personally expect to achieve by studying the package. In order to aid the communication between learners and the material it is important to include:

●   an introduction to the subject
●   advice on how long it will take to study the material
●   overviews of each subsection
●   summaries
●   conclusions
●   context-sensitive help.

Most of these devices should appear in all types of learning materials. They are intended to help learners understand the subject and indicate what they are trying to achieve. However, there is an important difference with computer-based learning materials – that is, an introduction to the computer system which is being used. This should be provided as an option at the start of the package so that repeat users are not forced to study the introduction more than once. The induction tutorial should cover issues such as:

●   input devices – new computer users may need assistance in understanding how to manipulate a mouse, keyboard, and so on
●   navigation of system
●   structure of material
●   meaning of icons.

Comparison of computer-based learning and traditional approaches

Communication is critical to the success of all forms of learning. Many traditional approaches are limited to the tutor addressing a group of learners with few opportunities for a genuine two-way dialogue. Computer-based learning, however, has the important potential to provide one-to-one individualized instruction.

Computers do not make value judgements of individuals so learners are free to work at the pace that meets their needs. Table 2.1 provides a comparison of computer-based with traditional approaches to learning.

The benefits of computer-based learning do not come about by accident. You must design the material to exploit the potential which CBL brings.

Table 2.1   *Comparison of CBL with traditional learning approaches*

Aspect	CBL	Traditional classroom
Tutor–student ratio	One-to-one	One-to-many
Tutor-to-student communication	One-to-one using online approaches	One-to-many with limited and occasional one-to-one
Student-to-tutor communication	One-to-one using online approaches	Restricted and limited
Student-to-student communication	One-to-one, one-to-many and many-to-many using online approaches	Limited communication
Individualized	Fundamental aspect	Normally not available due to high costs
Quality	Defined and consistent	Variable due to issues such as fatigue of tutor
Media	Text, sound, graphics, animation and video	Speech and visual aids
Learning process	Interactive and potentially individualized	Tends to be tutor-centred or initiated and focused on needs of the group
Flexibility	Provides the freedom to study at a time, pace and location of the students' choice but limited by access to computer equipment	Tends to prescribe the time and location of the learning event as well as influencing the pace of learning
Content	Determined by designer who must predict the needs of the learners accurately	Tutor has the freedom to include additional content at short notice
Cost	Reduces with number of students	Rises with number of students

Learner, subject and environment

Effective implementation of communication between learners and CBL depends on identifying the key factors in the relationship between learners, the subject and the learning environment. The relationship between the three sets of factors is complex. There are considerable differences between designing material for:

- a computer literate person compared to a newcomer to information and communication technology
- a person studying at home compared to someone working in a company learning centre
- a complex subject compared to a straightforward one
- adults with excellent communication skills compared to a group with limited basic skills.

Even simply considering one area shows that designing CBL for an environment with and without tutorial support is very different. The nature of the subject has a

Table 2.2   *Learner, subject and environment*

Learners' characteristics	Subjects	Learning environment
Age	Management	Workplace
Gender	Languages	Home
Motivation	Information technology	College
Computer literacy	Knowledge	Library
Learning style	Skills	Learning centre
Physiology (e.g. colour blindness, left/righthandedness etc.)	Attitude	Length of course
Motivation	New subject or revision	Individual learning
Basic skills	Vocational topic/skill	Within a group
Previous learning experiences	Competence	Human support (i.e. tutorial and general)

critical effect on the design of the material, the nature of communication and inter-action. A factual subject where the main objective is to acquire information is going to be different from a package aimed at developing a skill or changing learners' attitudes.

When designing CBL it is important to identify the key factors and consider how they relate and interact with each other. The learners' characteristics are not simply limited to physical attributes but also include their experience of and skills in learning. The subject covers both the content and nature of the objectives (that is, improving knowledge of a subject, developing a skill or changing an attitude), while environment is again both the location and learning structure (for example, degree of tutorial support and length of the programme).

Table 2.2 shows some examples of key factors of learners, subjects and environ-ments. Any factor in column one can be combined with any factor in columns two and three. This makes analysis difficult but also shows the importance of consider-ing the learners, subject and environment together.

Example
The following example considers the factors:

1. Young inexperienced learners will have limited prior knowledge and experi-ence of customer relations.
2. The material must explain why customer relations are important to the learners and the business. In other words, the learners must be motivated to study the content. The content will probably need to cover the fundamentals as well as the practical aspects of the subject.
3. The learners will access the package in the company learning centre where only general non-subject specific support is available, so learners need to be given a telephone number or e-mail address to obtain expert support. A young inexperienced person, however, may be reluctant to ask for help so some proactive mechanism is probably required.

This is a simple example and in practice you should discuss the situation with the learners themselves to test out these conclusions and investigate subject and environmental factors. Each factor provides a different degree of constraint and a challenge for the designer.

Communication styles

The term 'communication style' is a general expression for the way systems are designed in order for learners to interact or communicate with them. Many different styles have been developed for particular tasks and users. Most are used for purposes other than learning. Several styles have been defined as standards but often a mixture of styles is employed. The communication standards which are important to computer-based learning materials are:

- commands
- menus
- question and answer
- form fill
- direct manipulation
- natural language.

For computer-based learning systems it is important to realize that the communication style has the potential to aid or hinder the effectiveness of the material. Most learning material is only used by learners a limited number of times so that a style which is difficult to master is likely to hide much of the learning content. It is important that learners quickly assimilate the style so that they can efficiently navigate the material. Modern computer applications are often designed so that users gradually develop an understanding of their features, commands and structures. This is unsuitable for most computer-based learning since learners will be prevented from immediately accessing all the content.

It is good practice to provide a short introduction to your chosen communication styles (for example, explaining structure, icons, menus and headings). This should be an optional extra since it is very frustrating to be made to study it each time you return to a package.

Commands

Command style communication was the original approach to controlling computer systems. Users enter commands directly into the computer in the form of a word, abbreviations, single or multiple key presses (for example, q for quit).

This is a very efficient approach to control a computer system but it does require the user to memorize a range of commands. It is therefore important that they are meaningful so that the user finds them easy to remember. It is equally important that the user is skilled in the command syntax. This is the system equivalent of knowing your English grammar. The command syntax can be difficult to understand and occasional users often find it bewildering so it is essential that it is not the only method of communicating with the system.

Command systems are most suitable for users who already know the commands and syntax. For many computer-based learning products you will not wish to distract learners from the content by asking them initially to learn a set of commands. However, if the system requires only a small number of commands or if learners are likely to use the system extensively they can easily develop an understanding of the communication style commands.

A common command approach is the provision of a short cut by pressing a key such as Alt in combination with the first letter of the command (for example, Alt c for copy). This is effective unless you have several commands beginning with the same letter (for example, Alt p for paste and Alt w for print). Short cuts are often combined with other communication styles to provide an alternative choice for learners. This allows individuals who are familiar with the package quickly to locate the activity they wish to use. Less experienced learners can use menus which require little familiarity with the structure to navigate.

Logo is a command language intended to help students to explore geometry by providing a microworld in which a series of commands controls a pen. By manipulating the pen, students can draw geometric shapes (for example, triangles, rectangles, lines and squares). The logo commands are:

PU – Pen up (pen is raised above surface so that no mark can be made)
PD – Pen down (pen is lowered onto the surface)
FD – Forward (pen moves up the screen drawing a line)
BK – Back (pen moves down the screen drawing a line)
RT – Right (pen turns to the right)
LT – Left (pen turns to the left)
End – Stop

In addition the learners can use them to create new commands. For example:

Box (creates a square of side 100)

TO BOX

PD
FD 100 (forward 100)
RT 90 (turn through 90 degrees)
FD 100
RT 90
FD 100
RT 90
FD 100
END

The guidelines for designing commands for a learning system are:

- Make commands meaningful to the learner.
- Use a consistent syntax, abbreviations and short cuts.
- Keep the structure simple.
- Limit the number of commands.

Computer-based learning rarely uses a command communication style unless it is provided as an alternative (for example, short cut) to another style.

Menus

There are various menu systems and they have the great advantage that you do not have to remember the commands but simply locate them on the menu. Learners find menus easy to use because they do not have to learn the commands before concentrating on the learning material. However, the commands must be meaningful and the menu structure intuitive so that learners can locate them easily.

Permanent menus

Permanent menus (see Figure 2.1) take up valuable display space but since they are always visible they avoid the problem of learners becoming confused. In environments which may confuse such as web-based (hypertext) material, this may be especially important. If you need to minimize learning about the communication style, permanent menus could be the answer.

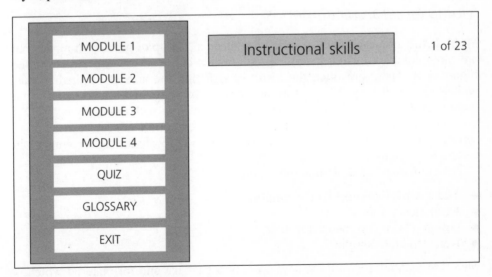

Figure 2.1   Permanent menu

Pop-up and pull-down menus

Pop-up and pull-down menus (see Figure 2.2) attempt to provide menu systems without taking up display space. Menus are limited to a toolbar, button or icon. Learners need to be aware that clicking on a button or icon will lead them to a whole list of options. For those experienced in using modern operating systems such as Microsoft Windows this is not likely to be a problem. Learners with limited computer experience, however, will need to gain an understanding of the communication style before they can study the material effectively.

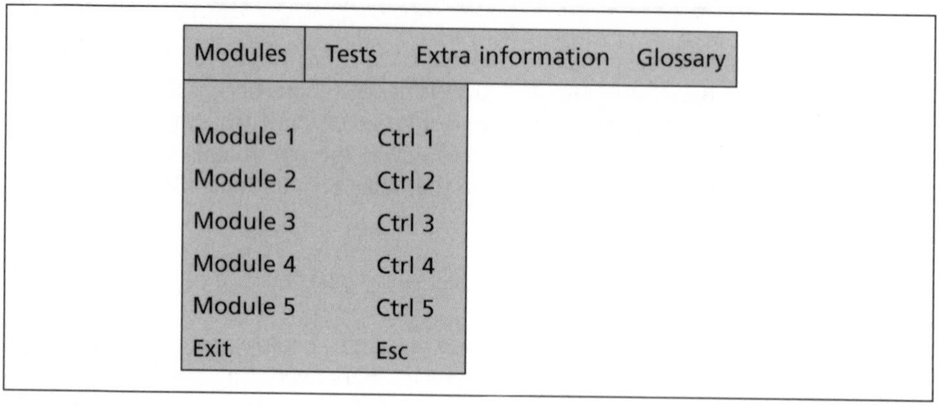

Modules	Tests	Extra information	Glossary
Module 1	Ctrl 1		
Module 2	Ctrl 2		
Module 3	Ctrl 3		
Module 4	Ctrl 4		
Module 5	Ctrl 5		
Exit	Esc		

Figure 2.2   Pull-down menu

Multiple/hierarchical menus

Multiple/hierarchical menus may be presented as pop-up or pull-down menus but are more complex in that individual commands can lead to further menus (see Figure 2.3). These are often the result of reducing the size of original menus, which were over-long. By limiting the number of items in a single menu to no more than seven you will avoid overloading the learner with too many options. If you need to exceed this amount then group related commands and use a line to separate different groups. For learners, the issue is to locate the right command in a complex structure.

The guidelines for designing menus are:

● Make items (commands) meaningful.
● Keep menus short.
● Group related commands together.
● Keep structure simple.

Menus are straightforward for new users of a package and for material which is likely to be used only a limited number of times they are probably a good choice.

| Modules | Tests | Extra information | Glossary |

Module 1	Ctrl 1
Module 2	Ctrl 2
Module 3	Ctrl 3 ▶	Section 1	F1
Module 4	Ctrl 4	Section 2	F2
Module 5	Ctrl 5	Section 3	F3
Exit	Esc

Figure 2.3   Hierarchical menu

Question and answer

Question and answer is a communication style based on generating a dialogue between learners and the system. Learners are asked a question and, based on their response, the system presents another question or displays content suitable for them (see Figure 2.4). This is often used to tailor information to meet the precise needs of learners or to provide them with specific guidance.

A simple form of question and answer would be to present learners with a series of single choices so that the material can be precisely customized to meet the individual's needs. Figure 2.5 shows a simple question where learners are asked to

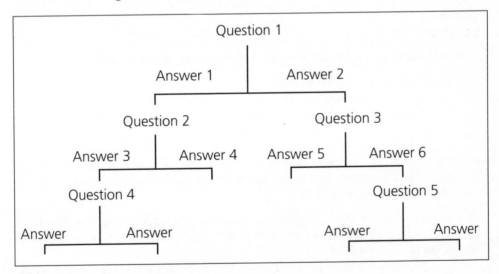

Figure 2.4   Question and answer dialogue

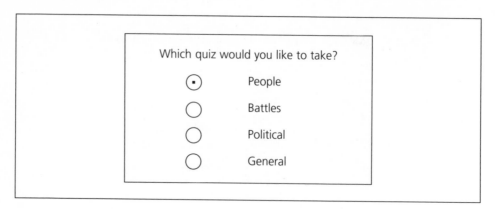

Figure 2.5   Customization

click on a radio button to choose between four different tests. This type of approach provides comprehensive options for learners. However, the more options and the more complex the structure, the greater the difficulty for learners to make an informed choice.

Question and answer is a very useful communication style to customize material, but it is unlikely to be suitable for an entire package unless its main aim is to provide individual advice and guidance (for example, careers information or an expert system).

Question and answer styles can be used to create role plays. Learners are asked to take on a role such as a manager undertaking an appraisal interview. Questions are asked to determine their approach and, depending on their answer, the computer-based learning offers feedback.

Example
Question:

> How would you begin the interview? (Select from the options below.)
>
> a)   by trying to put the individual at ease
> b)   by telling the individual what they had done well during the year
> c)   *by telling the individual what they had done poorly during the year.*

Feedback:

> People will often react badly to criticism; therefore it is often best to mix praise and criticism so that the individual realizes you are presenting a fair and balanced view of them.

Role plays based on a series of questions, answers and feedback may be illustrated by pictures or short sequences of video to show the outcomes of selections or to set the question in context.

The guidelines for designing a question and answer structure for a learning system are:

- Keep the structure simple.
- Use clear unambiguous questions and answers.
- Avoid complex nested questions.

Form fill

When learners are required to enter a variety of information into a system it may be useful to design the display to look like a form. As they fill in the form they move between its different parts by using a TAB key or by clicking on the next field.

In a learning system, form fill tends to be used in assessment tests, feedback forms, student registration components and search facilities. Outside of learning material the form fill style is more often used to enter repetitive information such as names and addresses.

Example
1. Assessment
   Fill in the blanks:
   Sodium chloride is often called _____ salt.

2. Student registration (see Figure 2.6)

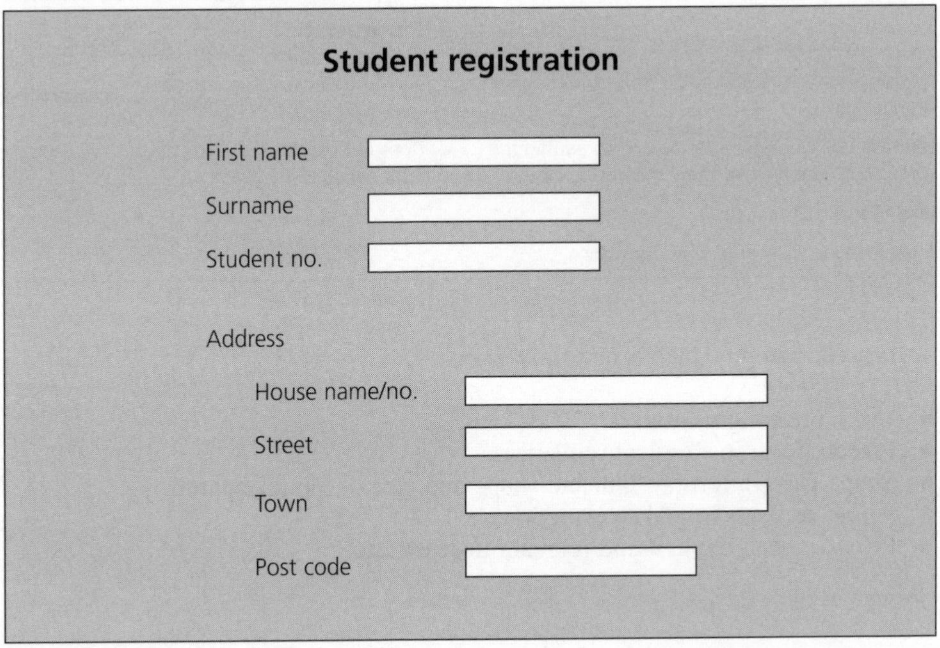

Student registration

First name

Surname

Student no.

Address

House name/no.

Street

Town

Post code

Figure 2.6   **Student registration**

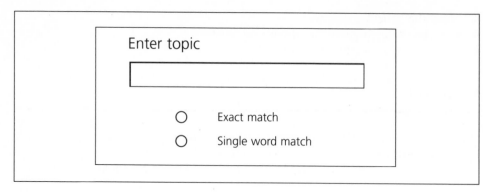

Figure 2.7   **Search engine**

3. Search engine
   Search engines (see Figure 2.7) are commonly associated with the Internet and with finding information on a large website. However, they are also useful in searching learning materials containing large volumes of information.

Table 2.3 presents the advantages and disadvantages of form fill communication styles.

Table 2.3   *Advantages and disadvantages of form fill*

Advantages	Disadvantages
Obvious which type of data is required (e.g. words, numbers etc.)	Very limited type of interaction
Learners do not have to position cursor within the form, so do not have to study the display closely	Does not facilitate presentation of information
Easy to make corrections	
Most learners are familiar with forms	

Basic design guidance is as follows:

- Use a meaningful title.
- Present form in a logical sequence.
- Shape gaps in form to indicate shape and size of input required.
- Allow students to make corrections.
- Provide clear, explicit and relevant instructions.

Direct manipulation

Direct manipulation represents the interface as a series of visual objects which the learners can manipulate using a mouse or other pointing device. It should be simple, natural and direct. Figure 2.8 shows a simulation of a convex lens. The learners can manipulate the lens by dragging it with the mouse pointer to drag it into different shapes and observing the changing focal point. They can experiment with a wide range of lens shapes (thinner and thicker) in any order to gain a clear view of how a lens focuses light.

Direct manipulation is suitable for both new and experienced computer users because there is less to remember in mastering the communication style. In our example simulation learners would only need to be able to use a mouse. Users would rapidly gain confidence, feel in control of the system and be able to predict system responses.

Direct manipulation can be used in different learning situations, for example:

- assessment (dragging answers to questions)
- simulation (identifying health and safety hazards within an environment).

Many modern computer applications include some degree of direct manipulation so experienced computer users are likely to be able to use this communication style and may even expect to be presented with it.

Direct manipulation systems should:

- be visible – objects appear on the display which can be moved, manipulated and used to control actions
- be reversible – they must allow learners to make mistakes and then retrace their steps to escape (often the systems have undo and redo options). It is important that learners are free to explore without the fear of getting lost or stuck
- use icons to represent objects
- allow a pointer to manipulate objects
- employ a familiar metaphor to help the learners predict the nature of the interaction.

Natural language

Natural language means that you are communicating with the system through your national language (for example, English) usually by typing the language into the system. This appears to promise a flexible and easy method of communicating since learners will already know their language. There are a number of limitations however:

- Variations – can the system cope with different spellings, punctuation and grammar?

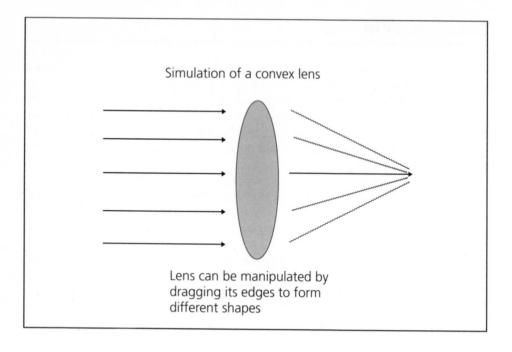

Simulation of a convex lens

Lens can be manipulated by
dragging its edges to form
different shapes

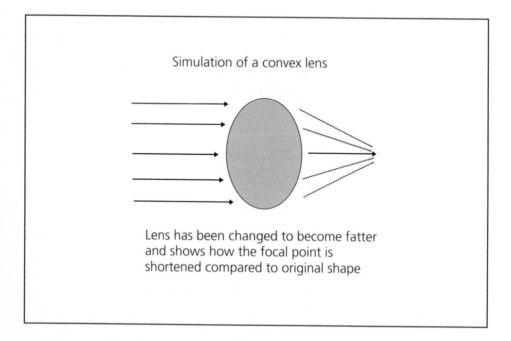

Simulation of a convex lens

Lens has been changed to become fatter
and shows how the focal point is
shortened compared to original shape

Figure 2.8   Direct manipulation

- Vagueness – people express themselves in many different ways. Can the system understand all the permutations?
- Ambiguity – language is often ambiguous. Can the system understand?
- Errors – people make typing mistakes. Can the system cope with errors?

One way to avoid or limit these problems is to allow only a small portion of the language to be used to communicate with the system. This would mean learners would need to remember what the system is able to understand and so the advantages of natural language would be reduced.

A spoken natural language style would raise the problems of accent, intonation and vocabulary. This would add to the possibilities of error and the system misunderstanding the learners' input. Speech input systems often require the users to train them to their voices which can take a significant amount of time. If the learner is prevented from immediately studying the subject by the need to train the system to their voices they are unlikely to find it a motivational experience.

The cost of developing a bespoke natural language style is high so it is unlikely that a designer will be asked to produce a new one. However, you may need to incorporate a commercially available natural language product into your package. Some key issues a designer will need to consider in selecting a suitable product are:

- Reliability – how often does the application fail to recognize a word, phrase etc? A failure rate of only 5 per cent can be very frustrating for users
- Training – does the system need to be trained to an individual's voice so that access is limited and learners are forced to undertake an extra task not directly linked to their learning objectives?

Although this may all seem very limiting, natural language plays an important role. It allow learners with limited basic skills to use computer-based learning materials which would otherwise not be available to them.

Summary of communication styles

Table 2.4 provides a comparison of the different features of the main communication styles. Although the descriptions of these styles appear to segregate them from each other it is normal practice to combine them to form an effective system which allows their best features to be employed together.

A computer-based learning product could use a form fill style to register learners, menus and direct manipulation to communicate with the tutorial, question and answer to provide help and guidance, and commands to control a small integrated simulation. This is an extreme case and would need to be designed carefully in order to avoid confusing and overloading the learners. Better practice is to limit the range of styles to perhaps two or three.

Many software producers (for example, Microsoft, IBM and Apple) have developed and published style guides which provide detailed advice on their

Table 2.4   *Summary of communication styles*

Communication styles	Description	Users
Command	Fast and efficient control system provided the user has memorized the commands	Only likely to be suitable for experienced computer users Probably only suitable for packages where learners will be repeat users
Menu	Effective control system based on recognizing options rather than remembering them	Suitable for inexperienced or occasional users of the learning material
Question and answer	Effective for straightforward interactions and for developing role plays	Suitable for most learners since it minimizes prior experience of the style
Form fill	Efficient input control system	Quick to learn but may be monotonous if learners have to use it a great deal
Natural language	Currently limited to a defined vocabulary and grammar but does have the potential to provide a natural style	Learners need to memorize the vocabulary and grammar
Direct manipulation	Natural actions (e.g. pointing and dragging objects) combined with highly visible interface	Potentially motivating and easy to learn since it is based on users' prior experience Suitable for most users

interface design standards. These help you to create communication styles that look and feel like the standard applications in which your learners may be experts and that allow your learners to use the materials quickly and efficiently.

Metaphor

A metaphor is a way of describing a new object by making connections with a familiar one. It allows learners to transfer their understanding from the old object to the new. This is very useful in interface design since the users can anticipate how it will work in terms of their existing experience. For example:

waste basket	– remove files
hour glass	– wait for an operation to be completed
magnifying glass	– zoom in
scissors and paste pot	– move objects around.

Microsoft® Windows® and Macintosh® operating systems use familiar objects to help users to recognize them intuitively. The users can understand the purpose of the functions by drawing on their knowledge of the metaphor.

Metaphors are an effective method of assisting learners to communicate with and navigate the learning material. They can be used with all communication styles. Metaphors provide a framework to show learners what facilities are available and how to access them. A metaphor based on a building allows the learners to predict that the library will hold additional information, the common room will offer communication links with other students, the lecture theatre will provide tutorial material, while the reception will provide access to other rooms and their functions. This saves the learners having to familiarize themselves with the system before they can use it effectively and efficiently.

A wide variety of metaphors have been used in the design of computer-based learning. Some possibilities include:

- schools
- training centres
- books
- library shelves
- solar system.

The key to success is to select a metaphor which is appropriate to the subject being studied and familiar to the learners.

Example
A tutorial on computer viruses could use a metaphor of a battle between two armies. The use of software to prevent infection could be compared to defences such as fortresses, trenches and barbed wire, while the restoration of the system could be compared to an army on the offensive.

Other examples are tutorials on:

1. the heart using the metaphor of a pump
2. geography using the metaphor of an atlas
3. English using the metaphor of a stage play.

It is important to consider what metaphor will work best with the subject and learners. Avoid over-complex metaphors – keep it simple and obvious. You could use different metaphors for different aspects of the subject but it is wise to test all metaphors with a sample of the learners. CBL is a visual learning method so metaphors which can be represented visually are often effective.

Summary of key points

General design issues

- Give learners a clear picture of the learning materials in terms of what they will be able to do when they have completed studying the package.

- Computer-based learning is very different from conventional learning materials and simply transferring good practice from other media is not likely to be effective.
- Consider the learners, subject and learning environment both separately and mutually in order to design effective computer-based learning materials.

Communication styles

- Communication style is a way of describing the different methods in which learners can interact with the learning material.
- The main computer-based learning communication styles are: commands, menus, question and answer, form fill, direct manipulation and natural language.
- Commands are a direct way of controlling the computer-based learning. However, they do require learners to understand the commands before they can effectively use the system.
- There is a wide range of different menu systems. They have the great advantage that the learners do not have to remember the commands but simply locate them on the menu. Learners immediately begin to use the system and to study the material.
- Question and answer is based on a dialogue between the learners and the system. Learners are asked questions and, based on their responses, the system presents another question or displays content suitable for them. The system takes account of learners' precise requirements. Material can be customized or specific assistance can be provided.
- Form fill is normally used to allow large volumes of standard data to be entered into a computer system efficiently. However, in education and training we often have to record information on individual learners so it tends to be used for that or similar purposes.
- Direct manipulation is suitable for all learners in that there is less to remember in mastering the communication style.
- Direct manipulation provides a natural style of communication allowing learners the maximum freedom to explore the material.
- Communicating with the system using your national language is called natural language style. This seems to be the ideal way of interacting with the learning material. However, the nature of language and the limitations of current technology limit its effectiveness.

Metaphor

- A metaphor is a way of describing a new object by making links with one which is familiar to the learner (for example, describing the human heart in terms of a mechanical pump). This helps learners to transfer their understanding of the familiar object to the new one.

Chapter 3

Types of computer-based learning material

By the end of this chapter you will have been introduced to a wide range of different types of computer-based learning material.

Types of material

Computer-based learning (CBL) can take a wide variety of forms depending on the design strategy adopted (for example, hypertext), medium employed (for example, video) and delivery approach taken (for example, online).

The main types are:

- computer-based training (CBT)
- computer-managed learning (CML) or managed learning environments (MLE)
- integrated learning systems (ILS)
- intelligent tutoring systems (ITS)
- job aids or electronic performance support system (EPSS)
- computer-aided assessment (CAA)
- drill and practice
- virtual reality (VR)
- multimedia
- hypermedia
- online learning
- resource-based learning
- simulation.

All these different approaches have been successfully used to deliver quality learning experiences on their own. However in many cases they have been combined to bring together the advantages of several types of CBL so that:

- the richness of hypermedia can be added to CBT
- assessment can be added to all the approaches
- materials can be delivered online
- simulation can be used to extend a computer-based tutorial
- multimedia can be used to help motivate learners being assessed.

There are few limitations to the combinations except a lack of imagination on the part of the designer.

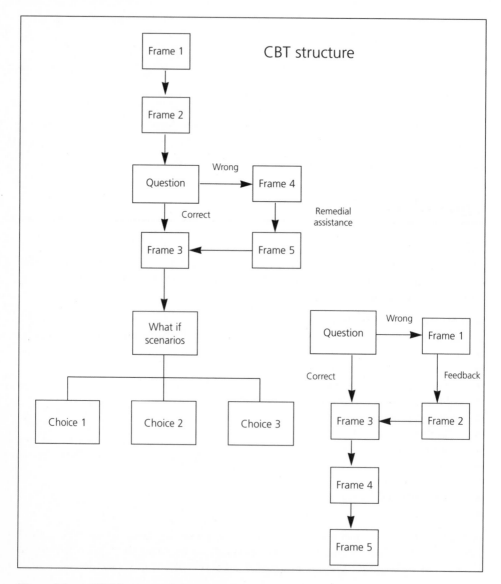

Figure 3.1   CBT frames and questions

Computer-based training (CBT)

Computer-based training (CBT) is sometimes referred to as computer-based instruction (CBI), computer-assisted instruction or computer-aided instruction (CAI). There is no clear difference between these materials, the names being largely the personal preference of the designer. CBT is often associated with a tutorial approach in that it presents a series of frames or screen displays of text, graphics and their combination. Each series of frames represents a discrete piece of content which is tested at regular intervals through questions (see Figure 3.1). The learner's response causes the material to branch so there are a variety of routes through the CBT. Each path is designed to provide a suitable learning experience for a particular group of people. There are many different ways of designing CBT however, and Figure 3.1 provides examples of three:

1. a tutorial with assessment questions included in the flow of the content with feedback loops
2. a structure based around asking the learners questions with the content determined by learners' answers
3. a choice of different options or scenarios for learners to explore. The learners can choose what is most appropriate for them.

The structure of CBT can be as complex or simple as the designer wishes. Figure

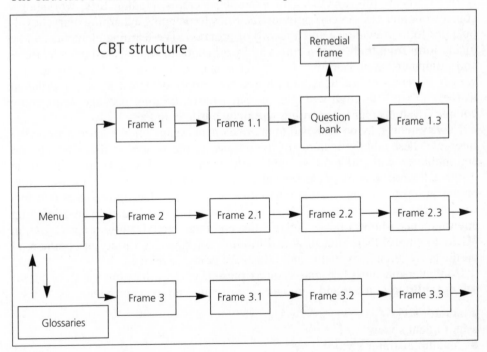

Figure 3.2   CBT structure

3.2 provides one example of a CBT structure. It can include many different features such as:

- glossaries of terms
- banks of questions
- different choices of route
- remedial help
- tutorial content employing a variety of media (for example, text, graphics, sound and images).

Computer-managed learning (CML) or managed learning environments (MLE)

Any course of study involves a wide range of activities including both learning, assessment and administration activities. These combine to provide learners with a rounded learning experience. Organizations who provide courses need to administer them. This large task involves registering hundreds or thousands of students, monitoring their progress in many different courses of varying length and components, checking if bills have been paid and collecting assessment evidence. From the learners' point of view they need to know their timetable, how the different course elements link together (for example, lectures, reading lists, workshops, coursework and assessment), provide facilities for keeping a learning diary, develop a portfolio of evidence and a record of progress. The learning elements can be in any form from traditional lectures and workshops to paper-based open learning and computer-based learning. Computer-managed learning systems come in a variety of levels of sophistication. Some are simply designed to help individual learners to work through a single computer-based training package while more complex systems manage learning within an entire college.

New systems may be designed to operate on an organization's intranet or on the Internet. These add the features of the intranet to the system so that students can communicate with their tutors, and each other as well as take part in online distance learning (for example, virtual seminars and mail groups). They also allow organizations to manage learning activities at a range of locations so that a virtual campus can be established. Online systems are often called managed learning environments. Many colleges, universities and large organizations are investing in MLEs to control their education and training activities. A variety of commercial products are already available and others are being developed.

Computer-managed learning systems present several different views of themselves to different users and complex sophisticated products provide:

- a tutor's view
- a student's view
- an administrator's view
- a technician's view.

Albert Gladstone		Tutorial Group – 3
Course: IT 345		Start Date: 12 - 09 - 2000 Finish Date: 15 - 06 - 2001
Participants	**Progress**	**Status**
Christine Murphy	overdue	P/T
Tom Haynes	average 64%	F/T
Peter King	average 78%	F/T
Carol Jones	resit	F/T
Harry Franks	average 58%	external
Sally Gordon	average 54%	staff

Figure 3.3   **Tutor's view of CML**

Christine Murphy 098765	Summary Record
Course: IT 345	Start Date: 12 - 09 - 2000 Finish Date: 15 - 06 - 2001
Modules	**Achievement**
1. Word-processing 235 2. Spreadsheets 457 3. Database 123 4. Search Techniques 5. Networks 876	Pass 56% Distinction 87% Course work overdue

Figure 3.4   **Student's view of CML**

The tutor's view (see Figure 3.3) provides them with tools to:

- monitor students' progress (both individual and the whole group)
- communicate with students
- present and structure learning materials
- mark online assignments
- plan their work.

The student's view (see Figure 3.4) provides them with tools to:

- manage their time
- monitor personal progress
- communicate with tutors and fellow students
- access information and guidance services
- develop a personal learning plan

- undertake self-assessment
- develop a portfolio of evidence for assessment.

The administrator's view provides them with tools to:

- produce management reports
- check enrolments
- check fees paid
- identify tutors' responsibilities
- obtain contact details for tutors and students.

Integrated learning systems (ILS)

Integrated learning systems (ILS) are a special form of CBL in which hundreds or even thousands of hours of learning material are combined. The material is controlled by a management system which assesses the learners' ability and presents them with appropriate content. As learners progress they are presented with more or less difficult material. The ILS adjusts automatically and continuously so that learners are always given appropriate material depending on their previous performance. They are therefore receiving individualized instruction.

The management system may be adjusted to control who can enrol, at what level and in which module they can begin. In addition, the system provides reports to help you monitor the learners' performance and maintains individual learners' records. Specific products may be able to provide other extra features.

ILSs are available for both children and adults and tend to concentrate on English, mathematics and science. They are reported to motivate users, especially learners with special needs. Some studies have suggested that learners can make substantial improvements in relatively short periods. Their use has been largely confined to schools and colleges.

Intelligent tutoring systems (ITS)

Intelligent tutoring systems (ITS) are designed to build expertise into learning material so that the student has access to an expert linked to a sophisticated learning system. They consist of four main functions:

- an understanding of learning methods so that learners can be presented with the right content, in an effective way and at a suitable speed
- expert knowledge of the subject in terms of good practice, factual and procedural knowledge and skills. This provides the content for instruction, standards of performance and examples of expert performance
- a model of the learner. This is developed by the system monitoring the learner's performance and allows the system to adjust its methods and approach to meet the learner's needs

- an interface between the system and the learner through which the instruction and interaction takes place.

An ITS should combine these four functions to provide individualized learning. The system will monitor progress so that a learner who is progressing too slowly can be automatically offered remedial assistance. The system will also adjust if the learner makes rapid progress.

Intelligent tutoring systems have largely been developed for research purposes and have not been extensively used outside of higher education.

Job aids or electronic performance support systems (EPSS)

Job aids are designed to support an individual in carrying out a new or occasional task. They are not new and many non-computer versions are available such as manuals, reference documents, handbooks, rule books and written procedures. Computer-based job aids are often called electronic performance support systems (EPSS) and are frequently designed to be used from the individual's desktop. They provide learners with aids whenever they are confronted with a new or occasional task so that they are able to perform the work satisfactorily. In a sense, training is available on demand or 'just in time'. Context sensitive help is a powerful support system in that it is available at the appropriate moment and is focused on the particular computer task being undertaken. It does not waste time showing material which is not useful at that moment. Computer applications are now being designed with extensive context sensitive help (for example, Microsoft Windows Help system).

EPSS can take a variety of forms including:

- expert systems which advise users on subjects outside their own experience
- checklists so that users are able to undertake occasional tasks in a systematic and correct way (for example, lists of questions to ask a caller to ensure all the required information is collected)
- short pieces of CBT to provide instruction in particular tasks
- focused good practice guides
- context sensitive help.

Intranets are ideal for holding a store of job aids so that individual employees can quickly access the material. Storing job aids on the organization's intranet also assists with keeping the material up to date since it is easy to access and change.

Computer-aided assessment (CAA)

One of the first uses of computer-based learning was the provision of quizzes on particular subjects. Often in the form of a large number of multiple choice questions, they allowed learners to test themselves as part of a revision programme. This approach is still common but computer-aided assessment has been extended to cover a number of other approaches including:

- psychometric tests
- question banks on particular subjects or systems to create banks
- learning styles assessment
- careers guidance systems
- systems to help learners identify their own skills and knowledge
- systems which allow tutors, assessors or individuals to record progress within a learning programme
- assessment included in a computer-based learning package (these are discussed in detail in Chapter 4).

In some cases computer-aided assessment simply transfers a paper test to a computer allowing marking to be automated and results to be available almost as soon as the test is completed. Using psychometric and similar tests as part of a selection process is a major advantage since marking by hand is often a slow process. Equally, marking some paper tests requires a skilled practitioner which makes self-use very difficult if not impossible. The computer allows these forms of assessment to be made available to the individual.

Guidance systems are still limited but do provide basic advice on complex issues, for example, the choice of a career. Packages can present individual users with the characteristics of different types of job to allow them to select what they would like to do. They can be linked to qualifications and experience required, possibly related to actual vacancies. Some systems attempt to analyse individual desires and preferences to match them to particular types of career.

An important type of computer-aided assessment product is one which is linked to the recording of progress towards a qualification. It allows individuals and organizations to monitor progress against the qualification standard and advise on the validity of the type of evidence and what needs to be done. The flexibility of many qualifications provides a range of routes to their achievement which can be combined making them complex to monitor. This is multiplied for organizations' training departments or colleges in that they often have many candidates. Systems which track progress are very useful.

Computer-aided assessment is rapidly developing in sophistication and, from relatively humble beginnings, is now evolving into a powerful tool.

Drill and practice

Drill and practice materials are often regarded as the poor relation of other CBL. However, they serve an important role in providing opportunities to practise skills. Learning is an active process and practice is vital. In a standard drill and practice

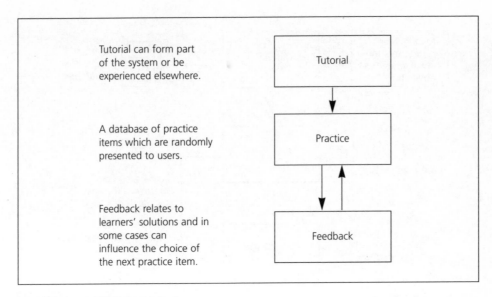

Tutorial can form part of the system or be experienced elsewhere.

Tutorial

A database of practice items which are randomly presented to users.

Practice

Feedback relates to learners' solutions and in some cases can influence the choice of the next practice item.

Feedback

Figure 3.5   Drill and practice

programme learners are presented with a short tutorial and then given a variety of opportunities to practice (see Figure 3.5). The practice is monitored by the system and feedback provided to aid the learners. For example, a package focused on using a mouse would explain the operation of the device and then provide practice on the different skills such as accurate movement, double clicking and dragging and dropping. The system would provide feedback, perhaps in the form of advice or a running score of how successful the learners had been. In some cases the initial tutorial is absent since the skills being practised have been experienced elsewhere.

Some drill and practice systems offer learners the choice of receiving guidance. This is very useful when learners are being asked to undertake a complex task with many related steps (for example, operating a process plant or carrying an accounts procedure with alternative routes and different options to consider). At each step the learners are provided with guidance on what are the choices, possible consequences and alternatives. In a sense they are being coached towards the correct decisions in a similar way to how a human coach would work. When learners are confident, they can choose to remove the guide and attempt the task on their own.

In practicing simple tasks guidance may be inappropriate. It will probably obscure the objectives and hinder the learners. A compromise is to provide the learners with an alternative to ask for a hint or tip when they are not sure of the next step.

Drill and practice packages are mainly used in subjects such as mathematics, English and computer input devices, but they can be used in any package which requires practice, the development of fluency and identification skills. Many tasks require learners to identify particular characteristics, such as viewing

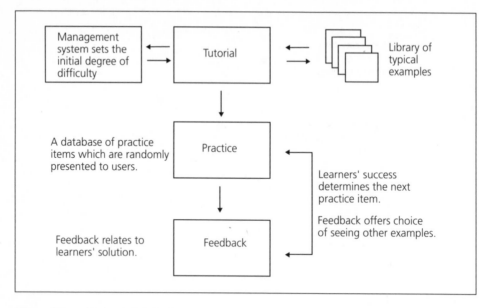

Figure 3.6   Enhanced drill and practice package

microscopic slides to select those showing abnormalities. In this type of task the majority of slides are free of problems and the abnormal characteristics take a variety of forms. It is therefore vital to provide controlled practice so that learners can experience in a few hours what would take months and perhaps years on-the-job. Equally importantly the learners are able to demonstrate competence in selecting the abnormal slides before they start their work. The feedback in this case could develop knowledge of the subject perhaps by showing different views of the same abnormality. Figure 3.6 shows a possible structure for this type of drill and practice programme. Structuring practice should include:

- identification
- selecting from lists
- ordering of sequences
- filling gaps
- eye and hand co-ordination.

Context

Drill and practice packages can be substantially improved by designing the material within an appropriate context. This will motivate learners to practise the less interesting aspects of learning. We could embody the mouse package we considered earlier within a jigsaw task in which the learners need to identify the correct piece by clicking on it, dragging the piece to the appropriate place and releasing it. The degree of difficulty could be varied, actions timed and a number of different jigsaws used to provide a variety of situation for continued practice. Many ICT tutors ask new computer users to play electronic card games (for example, Solitaire) to practise mouse skills. Most users find this more interesting than simply practising the skills without a context.

Speed

The speed at which a task is performed is often a key feature of mastery. The designer of a drill and practice package must decide on the time allowed to perform the tasks. Many packages gradually decrease the time allowed for a set objective or provide feedback on the time taken, sometimes by comparing a learner's performance with previous users (for example, 'You are currently the 11th fastest learner'). Some users find the concept of a competition motivating and will work hard to beat the fastest learner.

Virtual reality

Virtual reality is the creation of an artificial three-dimensional world which learners can investigate in a similar way to a real environment. They are free to move forward or back, left or right, even stand on their heads and the VR world changes to show learners what would happen in the real situation. Almost any environment can be developed using VR, for example:

- an underwater pipeline where divers learn welding procedures without risk
- a microscopic pond world in which learners can explore the creatures that live in a seaside pool
- a train in which new drivers can practice their skills without the cost of providing a locomotive and a track
- a nuclear power plant where learners can familiarize themselves with engineering routines without health and safety concerns.

There are many types of virtual reality system but the two extremes are immersion and desktop systems.

Immersion

In an immersion virtual reality system learners wear a helmet with a visor and gloves or a whole body suit. The equipment has sensors that allow the learners to experience the virtual world. By moving their head and hands the learners control the environment. If they look down their view alters accordingly and the gloves allow them to pick up and move objects within the world.

Immersion VR is powerful and realistic but it is also very expensive to develop, can only be used by one learner at a time and the helmet and gloves may be uncomfortable to wear.

Desktop

A desktop VR shows the world on the computer screen. Learners explore the environment using a pointing device such as a space ball, roller ball or a mouse. This system may seem poor in comparison to immersion VR but it can be a very realistic and powerful way of presenting the world and works well with a large display. Interaction with the VR world is via the pointing device – objects can be picked up and moved, or doors opened and buildings explored. The view on the screen is designed to emulate what a person travelling through the world would see.

CBL is generally very effective at helping learners gain new information and understanding. It is less effective at changing learners' attitudes and developing skills. However, virtual reality is capable of aiding the acquisition of skills and of changing learners' attitudes, particularly in immersion VR systems, whereas desktop systems mainly develop learners' knowledge.

Multimedia

The computer allows many different media to be combined together to create engaging and motivating learning material. Multimedia is the term for the integration of a range of media including:

- graphics
- photographs
- video
- text
- sound
- speech
- animation.

In practice it is unlikely that multimedia learning materials will include the full range of media. It is very difficult to combine them without distracting and alienating the learners. Yet multimedia can motivate learners by providing an exciting experience with a considerable degree of interaction. A key issue is the achievement of a balance between creating an exciting display which motivates the learners without overwhelming them with information and stimuli. An exciting interface may well attract learners but if it is not underpinned by a sound learning structure, then little will be achieved. For example, graphics, text and animation can be used to present content, while video can be used for role play feedback.

Multimedia is useful when learning:

- practical skills. Video allows learners to see experts demonstrating their tasks
- foreign languages. Learners listen to first language speakers and practise speaking while hearing their own attempts alongside the native speech
- people skills. Video and audio providing learners with experience of:
  - interviewing
  - dealing with customers
  - negotiations
  - carrying out staff appraisals
- about objects which are normally not visible because they are too small or hidden from view, such as:
  - features on microscope slides
  - internal views of machinery using animation techniques.

The design of multimedia will be covered in more detail in Chapter 8.

Hypermedia

Hypertext is designed to provide links between different electronic documents. By clicking on a particular word or phrase learners move to a related piece of information. Figure 3.7 gives an example of a number of links connected to the battle of Chickamauga. Learners can choose to find out more about anything in the messages which interests them. For example, if you clicked on the name of a general it would take you to information about his life and career. This is similar to browsing through a library.

Hypertext is a powerful means of linking information. A variety of forms can be linked so that pictures, words, buttons and icons are used as connections to further information. Hypertext then becomes hypermedia. Pictures can relate to words and words to pictures. Hypermedia documents normally have multiple connections so that users are free to follow their interests. Learners click on links which then jump to the new position. The jump can be within a single document or to another part of the system. Learners often find it difficult to recognize where they have moved to and become lost. This can cause them to become anxious, which will obviously affect their learning. The solution is to provide a link back to the previous position and often a connection to the main display of the system. Links are indicated in some standard way (for example, underlining words, changing the shape of the mouse when it is over a link and highlighting a phrase). Other solutions include:

- limiting the depth so that no chunk of information is more than three links away from the main display
- providing an overview map of the system so learners can locate themselves
- providing a search engine to locate particular items of content
- providing a tracking system (for example, history files in a browser) so learners can see where they have been and are able to retrace their steps.

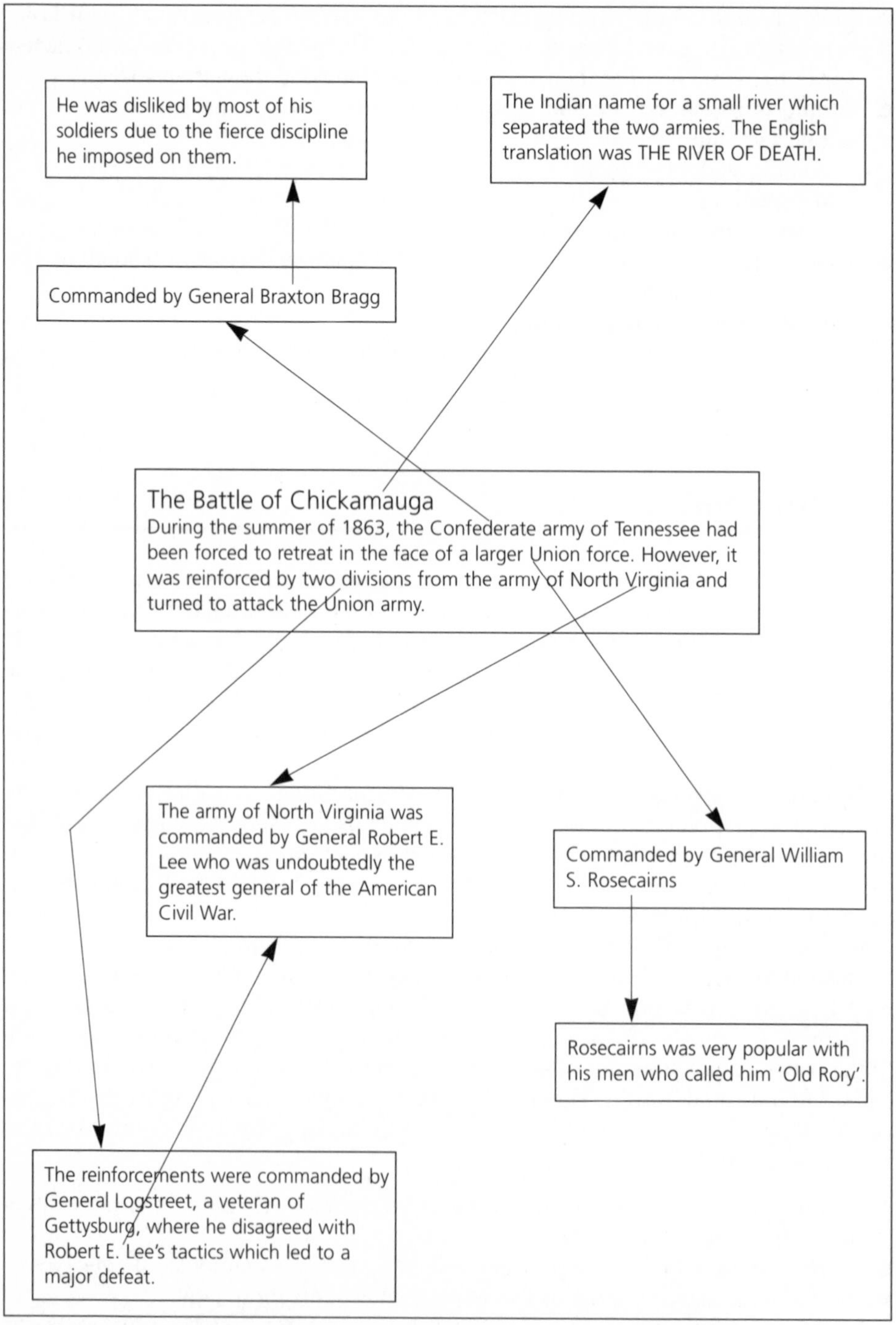

He was disliked by most of his soldiers due to the fierce discipline he imposed on them.

The Indian name for a small river which separated the two armies. The English translation was THE RIVER OF DEATH.

Commanded by General Braxton Bragg

The Battle of Chickamauga
During the summer of 1863, the Confederate army of Tennessee had been forced to retreat in the face of a larger Union force. However, it was reinforced by two divisions from the army of North Virginia and turned to attack the Union army.

The army of North Virginia was commanded by General Robert E. Lee who was undoubtedly the greatest general of the American Civil War.

Commanded by General William S. Rosecairns

Rosecairns was very popular with his men who called him 'Old Rory'.

The reinforcements were commanded by General Logstreet, a veteran of Gettysburg, where he disagreed with Robert E. Lee's tactics which led to a major defeat.

Figure 3.7   Hypertext

The type of interaction in a hypertext or hypermedia system may be described as browsing, exploring, scanning or touring. The difference between these labels is not precise but essentially they all suggest more choice for learners to study what they want to and ignore what they already know. There is a range of devices to aid these processes but the most effective is often called a guided tour. It offers a degree of structure in contrast to the completely free choice provided by the hypertext.

Guided tours provide a route through the hypertext from a particular perspective or in some cases a range of viewpoints. So a guided tour of Hampton Court could be from the following perspectives:

- Henry VIII
- a modern guide
- a lady in waiting.

In this way you can explore the information from several viewpoints, not just your own. A guided tour is a powerful stimulus to learning and overcomes many of the problems associated with being lost in hyperspace or simply being confused by the bewildering complexity and scope of information available. Guided tours provide paths through the information and aid engagement.

Online learning

Online learning is a general term which covers many different types of approach to the delivery of learning. The range includes:

- the simple downloading of a CBT package to your own computer, in effect acting as a high-speed postal system
- hypermedia tutorials available on websites
- enhanced communication between tutors and learners or between learners themselves to provide mutual support
- communication technologies allowing you to attend virtual seminars and to take part in conferences on other continents.

Figure 3.8 shows a learning environment which combines different approaches and features of the online world. Online learning is frequently expressed as overcoming the barriers of place, pace and time which many learners face. It provides learning at a place convenient for the learners to download material to their homes, desk or local learning centre; allows learners to study at the speed which is best for them; and offers learners the choice of when to study. The other important factor is that although computer-based learning attempts to provide a comprehensive package to individual learners, often additional assistance is needed. Communication technologies offer access to subject experts, other students and general support in an economic and efficient manner. E-mail allows a tutor to support a range of students at a distance while linking the students together so that they can help each other.

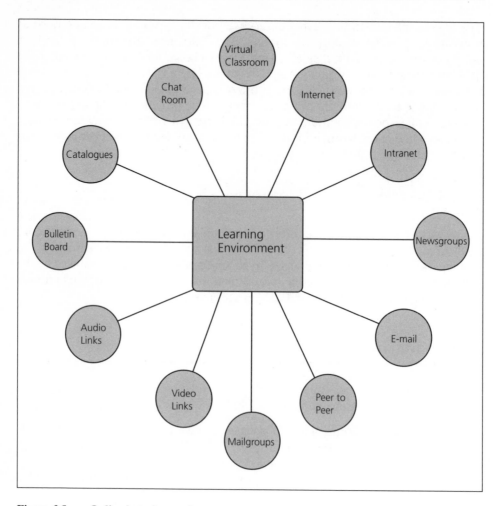

Figure 3.8   Online learning environment

A significant limitation of online learning is bandwidth. This is a measure of how much material can be sent or received through a particular communication route. In effect bandwidth determines the quantity and quality of material which can be employed online. A narrow bandwidth will prevent the use of a medium such as video since this involves large files of information which will take a considerable time to be transferred over the communication link. Even a short sequence of video (that is, one or two minutes) requires a large amount of band-width so that learners are forced to wait for some minutes before the sequence is run. This fragments the learning experience and probably breaks the individuals' concentration. Approaches such as reducing the size of files by limiting the frame rate have been used, but the quality of the video is also reduced. Streaming is the process by which the video is started before the whole file has been downloaded.

It reduces the waiting time but often the video is broken up and it is not a complete answer. Large files can be compressed to reduce their size and decompressed when received so that the downloading is considerably accelerated. However, quality is often affected by compression techniques. All these approaches are being continually improved, but bandwidth problems are likely to be with us for many years.

Within a single organization bandwidth is normally far greater than over public communication links so that sending online material to an individual's workplace is potentially not as restricted. However, although a network may have a large bandwidth it is shared amongst all users so the space available for sending multimedia may vary and performance will change. Networks within and without organizations are developing rapidly and bandwidth is increasing quickly. However, it is going to be several years before it ceases to be a limitation.

One way of overcoming bandwidth limitations combines CD-ROM technology with online methods to use the strengths of both techniques. Media which require a large bandwidth are stored on a CD-ROM which the learners play on their local computer. The CD-ROM links automatically to online materials that represent the more dynamic aspects of the content – that is, material which changes rapidly. It is relatively easy to update online material. CD-ROMs are excellent at storing large volumes of material. This combination provides a rich relevant content.

Resource-based learning

Resource-based material can take a variety of forms such as:

- manuals
- lecture notes
- book lists
- videos
- audio tapes and digital sound
- websites
- study guides
- photographs
- powerpoint slides
- workbooks and sheets
- open learning materials
- annotated references
- glossaries
- databases.

Resource-based learning is often associated with supporting or working in parallel with more traditional methods (for example, classroom courses). A conventional training course could be extended and improved by providing the trainees with extra learning materials. Technical trainees or apprentices can be given access to manuals, specifications and links to suppliers' websites in addition to workshop practice and classes. In higher education students would be given access to the lecture notes on the university intranet or the Internet. In this case the resource-based learning material is electronic text. This could be enhanced by providing a list of books, case studies and other material on the theme of the lecture.

Almost anything can be considered a resource. The whole of the Internet has the potential to be a learning resource. To turn it into a genuine learning resource requires some assessment of the content and establishment of links to particular learning objectives and courses. Thus websites which have been assessed for suitability and quality are an important resource in that each provides its own set of materials and information.

The benefits of learning from resource materials include:

- giving learners more control over their learning
- allowing learners to study at their own pace
- providing learners with the freedom to study when and how they prefer
- adding value to traditional methods.

Table 3.1 shows a comparison of a traditional approach with one enhanced by an additional learning resource. The addition of resource materials changes the traditional presentation to a more learner-centred approach, allowing learners more opportunity to ask questions and more freedom to study.

Table 3.1   *Comparison of traditional and resource-enhanced approaches*

Traditional approach	Traditional enhanced with resources
Presentation: one hour lecture using visual aids and a brief question period at the end	Seminar: one hour combining discussion, presentation and syndicate/small group activities
Materials: one or two handouts	Materials: self-study workbooks, frequently asked questions, reading lists, worked examples, assignments and lists of websites

Simulation

Simulations are a powerful aid to learning and are often associated with training in the use of complex equipment such as aeroplanes and control rooms. However, they are equally effective in providing an insight into more straightforward processes. Figure 3.9 shows a simulation for exploring whether substances can dissolve in water, acid or alkali. Learners undertake these three experiments without the risk of working with real acids and alkalis. Learners can test and compare a wide range of materials with each other and develop a reasonable understanding of the reactions. To carry out the same experiments would require an expensive laboratory, skilled supervision and careful health and safety arrangements. The computer simulation offers a means of reducing costs and providing new learning opportunities.

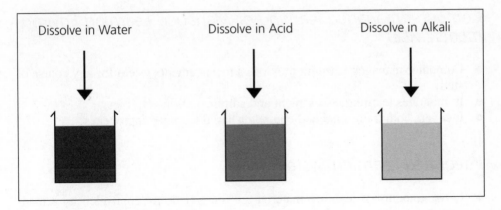

Figure 3.9   Example simulation

Simulations have two significant benefits over other learning methods:

- motivation
- transfer of learning.

Learners find simulations very motivating because they are active environments which are challenging. In our chemistry example we could have produced a tutorial explaining how each substance reacted to water, acid and alkali but a simulation is inherently more interesting to the learner in that it is active while the tutorial is essentially passive.

A key issue in any method is how well learners transfer their new knowledge and skills to new situations and in particular to the workplace. Simulations are very effective in transferring learning because they provide the learner with a context similar to the real one, thus helping them to decide which parts of their new experience should be used.

Simulations provide an exciting environment for learners to explore. However, it is important that learners know when they have discovered all the relevant facts. You must therefore provide clues within the simulation or clear guidance about what they should achieve, in the form of signposts, instructions, questions or a combination of these.

Summary of key points

Computer-based training (CBT)

- Computer-based learning is sometimes called computer-assisted instruction, computer-based instruction and computer-aided instruction.
- It frequently takes the form of tutorials, questions, feedback and differential routes based on learners' reactions to the material.

Computer-managed learning or Managed Learning Environments (MLE)

- Computer-managed learning provides a management system for any course of study.
- It integrates learning, assessment and administration activities.
- It covers both traditional and computer-based learning approaches.

Integrated Learning Systems (ILS)

- Large amounts of learning material are integrated and controlled by a management system.
- Systems assess learners' progress and present them with appropriate material.
- They are available for adults and children.
- They are often associated with English, mathematics and science.

Intelligent Tutoring Systems (ITS)

- ITS aim to provide individualized learning by combining expert knowledge of the subject, an understanding of learning methods, a model of the learner and an effective interface.

Job aids or Electronic Performance Support Systems (EPSS)

- These are available whenever learners need support with a new or occasional task.
- Training is available on demand or 'just in time'.

Computer-aided Assessment (CAA)

- CAA takes a variety of forms but is often associated with testing, guidance, recording of progress or a mix of functions.

Drill and practice

- Drill and practice presents learners with a short tutorial, and provides them with opportunities to practise and feedback on their performance.
- Some packages provide only practice of skills or knowledge learned elsewhere.
- Feedback can be linked to the type of practice provided.

Virtual Reality

- VR provides an artificial three-dimensional world for learners to explore.
- There are two main types: immersion and desktop.

Multimedia

- Multimedia integrates a range of media such as graphics, photographs, video, text, sound, speech and animation.

Hypermedia

- Hypermedia maximizes choice by making links between documents, pictures and other media.

Online Learning

- Online learning enhances communication between tutor with student and student with student.
- It gives high-speed delivery of materials to the place and at the time they are required.
- Bandwidth is often a key factor in designing online materials.

Resource-based Learning

- Resource-based learning is associated with supporting or working in parallel with more traditional methods.
- It adds value to traditional approaches by providing more learning opportunities.

Simulation

- Simulation allows training to be undertaken in hazardous environments.
- It motivates learners.
- It aids transfer of learning to new situations and workplaces.

Chapter 4

Assessment methods

By the end of this chapter you will have been introduced to:

- a wide range of assessment methods, in particular multiple choice, true or false and open questions
- reflective, reinforcing, self-assessment and engaging methods
- pre- and post-tests
- the importance of feedback.

Approaches to assessment

An important factor in any learning programme or material is the assessment of how much learning has been achieved. There are many different forms of assessment including:

- multiple choice and concealed multiple choice questions
- true or false questions
- open questions
- sequencing, sorting, classifying, ranking or ordering information
- matching
- gap or blank filling
- virtual trip or exploration
- role play using multimedia
- models and expert systems
- drag and drop
- bank of questions.

It is assumed that our interest in assessment is to gauge the effectiveness of using computer-based learning. However, assessments may also be considered when developing learning in other contexts. This is an important area since assessment is often difficult in all forms of training and education. Computers can offer objective, impartial and cost-effective assessment. Many conventional assessment processes are expensive because they require one or more trained assessors to undertake the process. Computer-based assessment is cost effective when used on a large scale since its unit costs fall with every user, whereas conventional costs tend to rise with more users (that is, you need more trained assessors).

In this chapter we will be considering computer-based assessment mainly as part of a computer-based learning package to test learners' progress. Remember that standalone assessment systems are useful to test knowledge, skills and competence learned elsewhere. There is considerable interest in these types of product.

Although all these assessment approaches will be presented separately they are frequently combined.

Assessment and other activities

Assessment in computer-based learning materials is not only about testing learners but also about helping them to further develop their skills and knowledge. Assessment activities should provide opportunities for learners to:

- reflect on the learning material and compare it with their previous experience and knowledge
- reinforce what they have been studying through exercises and assignments
- assess themselves
- be actively engaged in studying the learning material.

Assessments are a key source of interactivity which is a vital ingredient in the success of computer-based learning. Activities should be balanced so that a mixture of reflective, reinforcing and self-assessment exercises are included. These methods aid learning as well as assess progress.

The following are examples of reflective, reinforcing, self-assessment and engaging activities.

Reflection

Consider your previous experience of metals. How were they used and why? Write a list of their uses and identify one or more reasons why they were employed for the purpose.

This type of question is a powerful aid to learning because it encourages learners to review their previous experience of the subject (that is, metals) and to begin to make connections with the content of the tutorial. It engages the individual's mind and allows the new knowledge to be added to the existing resource. It is difficult to design a computer program that will judge this type of question since the answer is directly related to the learners' experience. Some will have extensive experience while others will have relatively little. The best way of assessing the answer is to allow the learners themselves to make the judgement. This is often done by providing a discussion of the answer so that they are able to compare their own responses with a standard.

Discussion

You may have many different experiences of the use of metal but some typical uses are:

Use	*Why?*
Car bodies	Metals are strong but easy to press into different shapes
Electrical cables	Metals conduct electricity and can be stretched into long strands
Nails	Metals are hard and strong
Tools	Metals are hard but can be shaped in a wide variety of forms
Cooking pots and pans	Metals conduct heat

Another approach is to provide the learners with a series of hints or tips which would help them to reflect on their own experience. If they were unable to see any connection between the question and their experience the hint would help them make the links. This is similar to what a tutor would do in face-to-face learning. It is also perfectly feasible to combine hints with a discussion of a standard answer.

Reinforcement

What are the main properties of metals we have discussed? Select from the list below all the main properties:

1. insulation
2. conduction
3. strength
4. lightness
5. flexibility.

The main role of a reinforcement question is to highlight the key learning points from a section of the material. This prevents learners from progressing without the key issues being understood. If the learners select the point that metals are insulators you can provide them with feedback that explains that metals are good conductors of heat and electricity and poor insulators. Designers will often use reflection type questions to gain the attention and interest of learners and employ reinforcement to check understanding at the end of each section. Both are frequently compulsory – learners are forced to attempt the questions before they can proceed.

Self-assessment

Learners in all situations need to know how they are progressing in order to maintain their interest and motivation, but because each person will have different needs in terms of self-assessment it is difficult to design one approach to fit all situations. A successful method is to provide an option at regular intervals throughout the learning material to undertake a self-test or quiz. The learners are able to select this when they need to check their own progress.

Engagement

All types of assessment should seek to engage the learner. Two useful approaches are:

- simulate a real situation in which learners try out their new understanding
- ask the learners to undertake a task away from the computer.

Example

Earlier you were asked to list the different uses of metals and explain why they are used. Now see if you can identify different metals being used for different purposes around your home or workplace. Take a short break while you walk around identifying the metals.

Respond to the learners' list in a similar way to a reflection question by providing a discussion of possible solutions:

Metal	*Use*
Copper	Electrical cable and coins
Aluminium	Pots and pans, and window frames
Steel	Spanners, screws, nails, nuts and bolts and cars

Pre- and post-tests

Two main means of assessment in computer-based learning are:

- pre-test, and
- post-test.

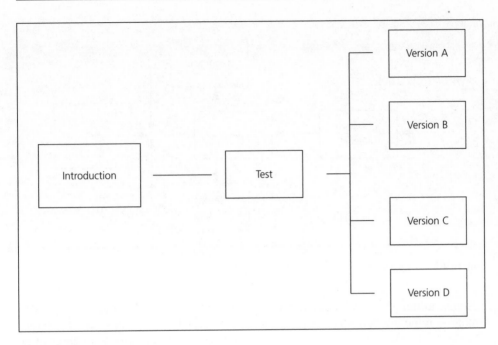

Figure 4.1   Pre-test

Pre-tests customize learning so that users are not asked to study material they have already demonstrated their competence in. The test is presented to the learners as soon as they begin the package. The system can adapt the learning material automatically depending on the results of the test. In practice many pre-tests do not provide this type of customization but simply allow the individual learners to self-assess in order to make informed choices of what to study (see Figure 4.1). This straightforward device is a main benefit of computer-based learning in that learners avoid being forced to duplicate their learning experience. Significant time-saving can be achieved compared with conventional learning experiences (for example, in a classroom all students are required to study the whole content of the course) and, in turn, costs. A pre-test that shows learners they are already competent in a subject is a very positive outcome. Too often learners return from a course to say that they already knew a large part of the content. A poor pre-test would be one which is not linked to the learning material – in other words, one that does not test understanding, aid the learners' choice of what to study or automatically customize the material.

Pre-tests are not merely concerned with assessing understanding of the material, they can be used for other purposes – for example, to identify the students' learning styles in order to present them with a version of the tutorial which is design to meet their learning preferences (see Figure 4.1).

Post-tests are in some ways far simpler in that they are intended to assess how much the learners have achieved by studying the tutorial. This type of summary

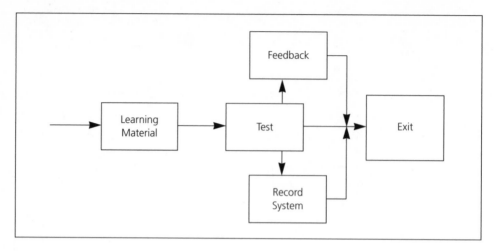

Figure 4.2   Post-test

activity, although valuable, is fairly limited. Value is added if the post-test also suggests remedial activities or revision to be undertaken to achieve a satisfactory standard (see Figure 4.2). However, they are low cost, straightforward and can be designed to reflect external standards.

Both pre- and post-tests can benefit from the accurate measurement of time which a computer can provide. Tests can be precisely timed or time limits imposed on the learners. It is also possible to present a clock on the screen to allow the learners to monitor themselves.

By applying both types of test it is possible to determine the effectiveness of the learning material by measuring both the learners' initial and final understanding.

Adaptive testing

Adaptive testing is based on having a resource bank of questions or test items with different degrees of difficulty. The levels of difficulty are carefully designed and the testing validated. The learners are presented with a question or test of medium difficulty. If they get it wrong they are presented with less difficult items until they are successful. If they get the initial question right they are offered more difficult items until they get one wrong. This process rapidly allows the system to assess the level of difficulty a learner can cope with.

Adaptive testing can assess learners quickly and effectively. However, it is essential to assess accurately the level of difficulty of each test item. Figure 4.3 shows the structure of adaptive testing. This approach may be useful as a pre-test because it can precisely customize the material to the individual learner.

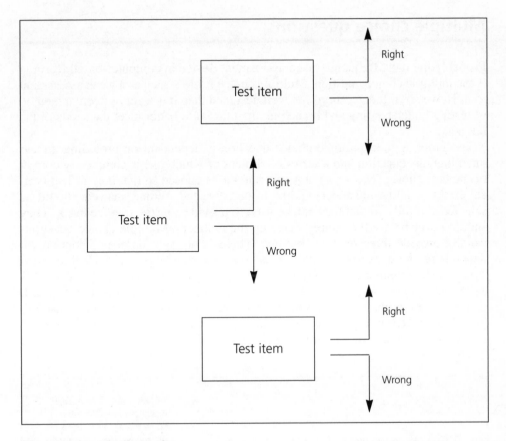

Figure 4.3   **Adaptive testing**

Feedback

A vital factor in computer-based learning assessment is the feedback that learners receive when they have answered the test. Feedback is as important as the question itself. Effective feedback should motivate the learners and help them to understand what they did wrong in order to get it right next time. Endlessly repeating 'have another go' is not sufficient. Equally, telling the learners 'well done' every time they get a question right is not tremendously motivating. Good practice is:

● explaining why the response is wrong
● praising correct answers and adding extra information as a sort of bonus
● using learners' errors to diagnose weaknesses and offering solutions
● employing a range of different types of feedback
● avoiding devices which might be associated with earlier failings at school such as crosses and ticks.

Multiple choice questions

Probably the most frequently used assessment device in computer-based learning is the multiple choice question. Multiple choice is often seen as a weak assessment tool. However, if the questions are well designed then it is a very effective method of testing understanding and branching the tutorial to better meet the needs of the learners.

Designing a good multiple choice question is dependent on providing a clear unambiguous question and a series of choices of which one is completely correct or the best choice. The wrong answers should be chosen so that they reflect typical errors or allow misunderstanding to be corrected. Wrong answers should be selected carefully so that they can be used to provide constructive feedback. They should never be used to simply make up the numbers. Multiple choice questions usually provide three or more options. There is no right number of options, it depends on the question and the typical misunderstandings you want to correct. You can allow learners more than one attempt at a multiple choice question. It is nevertheless poor practice to allow the learners so many attempts that they will gain the correct answer by repeatedly guessing. Multiple choice can be used to branch the material to provide assistance for learners who fail the test. Figure 4.4 provides an example of a multiple-choice question.

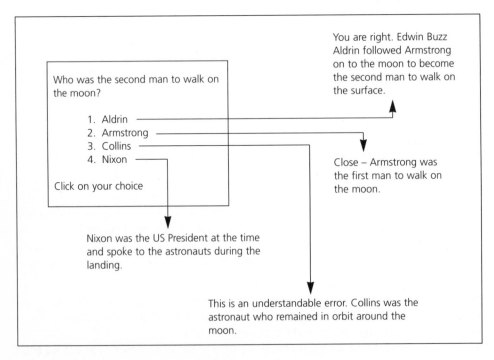

Figure 4.4   Multiple choice question

Multiple choice is effective when it is designed well. Questions should:

- be clear, concise and unambiguous
- vary the action you want the learners to take such as:
  - select the correct answer
  - select all the correct answers
  - select best answer
  - select wrong answer
- randomly position the correct answer in the choices
- select options so that you can provide useful feedback
- ask how, what, why, who and where
- use both pictures and text
- have more than three options
- represent each incorrect option as a common mistake or misconception
- avoid giving clues to the answer
- vary the feedback and not simply tell learners they are right or wrong.

Multiple choice is often criticized because it allows learners to guess the answer. One way of overcoming this weakness is to conceal the answers and reveal them one by one so that the learner must decide whether each separate answer is correct on its own. So the example shown in Figure 4.4 would be changed to Figure 4.5.

Concealed multiple choice is rarely used but it is an effective alternative to the more conventional approach if there is a problem with learners guessing the right answers.

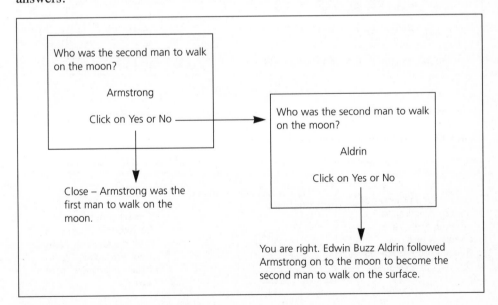

Figure 4.5   Concealed multiple choice

A more visual and perhaps motivating form of multiple choice is to provide the learners with a scenario (for example, a short video sequence, sound commentary or a slide show). After the show the learners are presented with a question related to the scenes and a series of answers. This is a useful approach to testing inter-personal skills (for example, interviewing, selling, telephone techniques and customer relations).

True/false questions

The simplest form of assessment is the true or false question. Learners have a 50/50 chance of success so it is inappropriate to allow more than one attempt at each question. True or false questions are frequently grouped together to offer a set of questions which will assess knowledge of a subject area (see Figure 4.6). Individual true or false questions are essentially a limited form of multiple choice.

It is more effective if a clear question is employed with adequate feedback. It is not enough to limit the response to the learner as right or wrong. Explain why the choice is wrong and add value to a correct answer (see Figure 4.7). This is

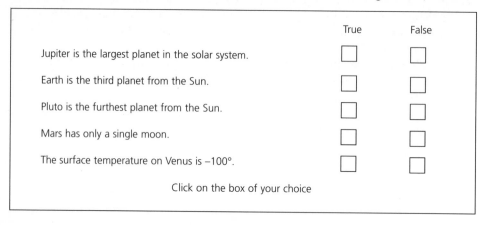

Figure 4.6   Set of true or false questions

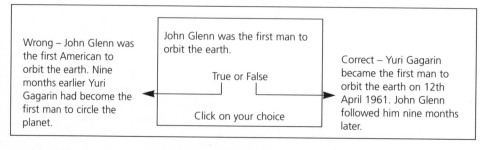

Figure 4.7   True or false question with feedback

particularly important in a situation where learners have a good chance of guessing the right answer.

Open questions

An open question is one which learners are free to answer in any way they feel is appropriate. This is a very useful way of assessing the learners' knowledge and understanding of a subject although it does have some weaknesses for computer-based learning. It is very difficult to design an automatic way for the computer to mark the learners' responses without using imprecise approaches such as matching words. The designer selects a range of words which are regarded as typical and the computer program searches the answer for matches. If there are matches then the computer program gives feedback. However, often learners will use perfectly acceptable alternative words that the computer will ignore and hence give inappropriate feedback. A solution often adopted by designers is to use only open questions with short answers so that it is possible to match all the alternative words.

Examples of short open questions
What is the capital city of France?
What are the colours of the spectrum?
How many countries are members of the European Union?
Name four English cities.
Who is the President of the United States of America?

Standalone computer-based learning often avoids open questions because of the problem of judging the quality of the answer. However, by using communication technology it is possible to send open answers to a remote tutor who marks the answer and provides feedback to the learner. There is obviously a time delay between answering the question and receiving the feedback. Other assessment approaches are able to provide an immediate response to learners.

Open questions are more frequently used in paper-based distance learning where the problem of feedback is solved by using model answers or discussions in the form of lists of items which learners may have included in their answers. However, tutors are often employed to mark and provide feedback to open answers. This method of allowing learners to assess themselves by comparing their answer to a model one is rarely used in computer-based learning although it is perfectly sound.

Open questions can provide a focus for a group discussion while electronic conferences, mailgroups or chat rooms are able to provide the means. Answers take the form of contributions to the group debate while feedback would come from the response of the other students to an individual's views. This can be a useful self-assessment method as well as an alternative approach to learning.

Sequencing, sorting, classifying, ranking or ordering information

The importance of a particular item of information often rests in its relationship to other elements so that assessment of understanding needs to test the sequence, ranking or order in which the items appear. Computer-based learning is effective in asking learners to sort, rank or classify information. A program can check the sequence of presentation very easily and immediately give feedback to the individual on the degree of success or failure of the attempt.

Example
List the planets in the order of their distance from the sun starting with the closest and working to the furthest away:
    Neptune, Mars, Saturn, Earth, Pluto, Mercury, Jupiter, Venus and Uranus

First attempt:
    Venus, Mercury, Earth, Mars, Saturn, Neptune, Jupiter, Uranus and Pluto

Feedback:
    Venus, Mercury, Earth, Mars, Saturn, Neptune, Jupiter, Uranus and Pluto

Highlighting indicates the planets which are in the correct sequence. This feedback could be improved by also indicating the planets that are only one place away from their correct position.

This is a straightforward example but other subjects are suitable for some form of classification exercise. Many tasks have to be performed in a particular sequence. An important part of learning a job is to know the order in which each element is carried out.

Example
Arrange the following tasks in the correct order when changing a tyre on a car:

    Raise the car
    Switch on hazard warning lights
    Position spare tyre
    Park the car on firm level ground
    Place a rock or wedge to block wheel diagonally opposite to the one you are changing
    Locate and remove spare tyre and tools from the boot
    Locate jacking point on car
    Check you have all the required tools
    Loosen the nuts on the wheel
    Replace tyre
    Lower the car
    Tighten the wheel nuts

Put punctured tyre and tools away
Repair puncture.

There are often alternative sequences so it is important to identify all the different orders and provide appropriate feedback. There are few things more annoying to learners than to get a question right and be told it is wrong. This can seriously demotivate them. In this example there are a number of relatively minor changes of order of some tasks (for example, do you switch on the hazard warning lights before or after you park the car?). It is more important to be aware that there is widespread poor practice so the feedback should explain that some approaches are not best practice (for example, loosening the wheel nuts when the car is jacked up can rock the car and cause it to fall – a dangerous approach but one which unfortunately is used by many people).

Matching

Matching is an assessment method where learners are asked to pair different pieces of information together, such as linking capital cities with their countries or football players with their teams.

Example
Match the astronaut, the event and year:

Svetlana Savitskaya	First Space Walk	1971
Yuri Gagarin	First American Space Walk	1965
Valentina Tereshkova	First Drive on the Moon	1965
Alexei Leonov	First Woman Space Walk	1963
David Scott and James Irwin	First Woman in Space	1961
Edward H. White	First Man in Space	1984

This is a complex match in that there are three interrelated pieces of information. It is a real test of the learners' understanding. Feedback can be provided to tell the learner how many items are in the correct position.

Gap or blank filling

In a gap-filling assessment a short passage is provided on a subject in which a number of words or phrases have been removed. The learners are asked to fill in the blank spaces either with words of their own choosing or from a list provided. If the learners are free to use any words then you need to predict all the acceptable words or phrases so that the computer program can check if they are right. This is a more difficult test for the learners than selecting from a list, where you are essentially providing them with a set of clues. In practice you may wish to make assessment more or less difficult in different contexts.

Example

Information and .... technologies have the potential to overcome many of the barriers which people who are .... or .... disadvantaged encounter to access education and training. However, for ... to achieve this result adults need both the technology and the .... in how to use it. At the moment they often have neither, with computers more likely to be owned by younger and relatively .... men.

Fill in the gaps in the above using the list of words below:

> competence
> economically
> ICT
> communication
> affluent
> socially

You are free to provide clues such as indicating the size of words with dots.

Virtual trip or exploration

In dangerous environments (for example, nuclear plants, deep sea diving and chemical plants) it is very difficult to provide on-the-job assessments. Equally in situations where mistakes are expensive assessments are often impossible to conduct. However, staff need to be tested to ensure they are competent before they start work, to ensure that other staff are not at risk or that high costs will not be incurred. Computer-based learning can resolve this dilemma by using virtual reality techniques.

Virtual reality systems are not restricted to these extreme environments. They can be used in many other situations where you want the learners to experience a realistic environment as part of the learning experience and to have their skills and understanding tested in that situation.

Example of hazard spotting exercise

Create a virtual garage and ask learners to explore the environment in order to identify the health and safety issues. Each object in the garage could be examined to see if it present any risks. Unlike the real situation each piece of equipment could explain its purpose and how it should be used. Learners assess the information and make decisions and the virtual garage provides feedback which helps them to improve their risk assessment skills.

Role play using multimedia

In conventional learning, role plays are a powerful means of developing skills, understanding and competence. Many skills are based on observing a given situation, diagnosing the issues and deciding what to do. Multimedia allows learners to witness events, make decisions and see the consequences of their actions. This approach has been used extensively in the area of interpersonal skills training such as customer relations, interviewing and presentation skills.

Typically, learners are shown a short sequence of video depicting an event such as a confrontation between a manager and a member of staff. After viewing the scene learners are asked to take the part of the manager or individual and decide from a range of options what they would do. After making their selection they are shown a second sequence revealing the consequences of their decision. Learners can quickly see the outcome of their action. This type of approach allows learners to practise skills they have been studying and appraise themselves.

Models and expert systems

Computers can accurately simulate environments which can be scientifically modelled – for example, a chemical reaction in a process plant – in order to show the result of different operator actions. The skills and understanding of plant staff can be assessed in detail before they are used in the real situation. Models are very useful in environments where on-the-job training is inappropriate (for example, high risk, impracticable or expensive). In a process plant or power station it is difficult to demonstrate all potential scenarios because they rarely occur or are theoretical situations. Learners can be asked to carry out these operations or react to set problems while the model will respond according to their actions. This is a powerful way of testing learners' competence.

In a similar way expert systems provide an environment which is governed by a set of rules or interrelationships. These take a variety of forms but are particularly useful in areas of complex knowledge (for example, workings of a specific piece of equipment, stock exchange and the weather). An expert system works by inherence so that, given learners' responses to a situation, it can provide detailed feedback as well as assessing their knowledge.

Drag and drop

Computer systems commonly use pointing devices such as a mouse to manipulate objects on the screen. This provides opportunities to develop assessment exercises based on dragging objects to particular positions on the screen. These activities are called drag and drop. Figure 4.8 challenges learners to drag labels to their

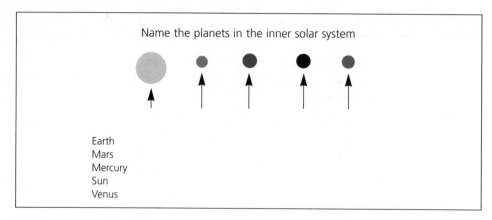

Figure 4.8   Drag and drop

appropriate positions on a diagram and drop them into place. If they are unsuc-
cessful the label returns to its original position allowing learners to try again. This
method provides immediate and accurate feedback to learners.

Bank of questions

Computers can store large numbers of questions making it relatively easy to
change the assessments in a computer-based learning package and enabling
learners to use the material many times without encountering the same tests. This
feature can be used to present assessments in an interesting and motivating way.
Figure 4.9 shows a bank of questions. Learners click on the square of their choice
and they are presented with a question. The bank can contain questions or assessment tasks of all types.

Other approaches

Many other computerized assessment methods have been successful including:

- storing and managing different examples or questions so that learners can
  practice before being tested

- presenting photographs, graphics, videos and other forms of illustration to
  individuals or groups of learners so they can identify selected points, objects
  or issues. This allows a wide range of environments to be tested without the
  burden of taking the learners to each location

- management games and simulations like those that have been used in classrooms or other conventional settings for many years. The computer adds both

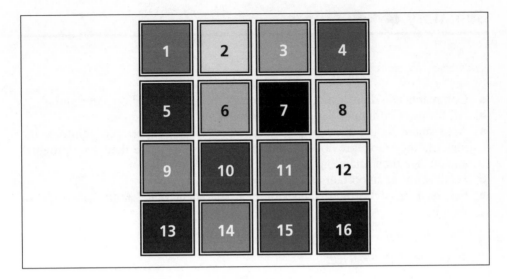

Figure 4.9   Question bank

to the realism of action and also to the speed of feedback, allowing learners to practice and assess decision-making and problem-solving skills

- language learning activities in which users can record their own efforts and compare them to an expert delivering the same spoken text. This is similar to but quicker than a conventional tape approach since tapes do not need to be rewound or changed over. It is a highly effective form of self-assessment

- digital video to capture practice of skills such as sign language

- communication technologies allowing a remote assessor to take part in tests which would otherwise be impossible or too expensive. Examples are testing computer skills by monitoring learners' work, observing learners using video conferencing and monitoring an online group discussion.

Maintenance

Currency of all questions and tests must be maintained. A single out-of-date item can seriously harm the credibility of the material. Learners will begin to doubt the validity of the assessments and this is a short step to deciding to stop and failing to complete the material. Maintenance requires a systematic and organized approach whereby all materials are reviewed regularly to check currency. This is rather like a planned maintenance programme for equipment. Often reviews are regarded as low priority but they are essential to maintain the acceptability of the computer-based learning.

Summary of key points

General issues

- Computers can deliver assessments for all forms of education and training.
- All forms of computer-based learning must include assessment.
- Assessment should allow learners to reflect on their experience, reinforce the material they have previously studied, help them to judge their own progress and engage their attention.
- Feedback is as important as the assessment.
- Feedback must be more than simply a statement that learners are right or wrong.

Assessment methods

- Pre-tests allow you to customize material.
- Multiple choice questions are very effective in both testing understanding and branching material according to the responses of the learners.
- Hidden multiple choice reduces the possibility of learners guessing the right answer.
- True/false questions can be effective if used in small groups and combined with good feedback.
- Open questions are difficult for a computer to mark due to range of possible answers, but can be successful if used in a limited way.
- Open questions can be effective if linked to communication technology so that a tutor can mark them and provide feedback.
- Sequencing, sorting, classifying and ordering tasks are very useful in testing relationships.
- Virtual trips or exploration help assess skills in environments which are hazardous or impracticable to use (for example, too expensive).
- Multimedia assesses competence in a realistic situation.
- Models present accurate environments for testing learners' understanding.
- Computers are able to store large numbers of questions so can provide considerable choice.
- Computers are able to deliver a large number of assessment approaches.

Maintenance

- Questions and tests must be kept up to date.

Chapter 5

Use of text

By the end of this chapter you will have been introduced to:

- the nature of a text display compared to a page
- the role of text in learning materials
- the communication approach of learning materials
- chunking, scrolling and justifying text
- the choice of text styles available to you
- newspaper techniques to aid readability
- combining text and graphics
- combining text and colour
- structured text
- communication devices to aid understanding.

Presentation of text

Although computer-based learning materials are often discussed in terms of the power of multimedia to deliver learning, text is still an important means of communicating with a learner and in many ways it is the most powerful. Presenting text on a screen is broadly similar to presenting it on the page, but there are a number of differences.

The quality of print on the screen is significantly poorer than that on a page. The quality of screen display is usually discussed in terms of resolution – that is, the maximum number of dots, or pixels, which make up images or text. Resolution has improved dramatically over the last ten years but is still inferior to an image or text printed on paper.

The screen and the page are both rectangles but the screen normally has less space than a page and has a landscape orientation whilst a page is normally portrait (see Figure 5.1). These differences of quality, size and orientation may seem

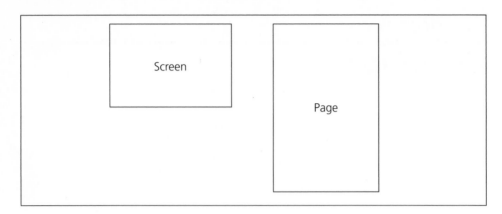

Figure 5.1   Orientation of screen and page

small but they have a great effect on the readability of text and the learners' willingness to read.

Reading large amounts of text on a screen is more difficult and unpleasant than from a page, so if you need to present large volumes of text it is probably better to include a workbook in the learning package. Text on a page is normally black type on a white background. The screen on the other hand offers a range of foreground and background colours.

Learners read text on a screen more slowly than they do from a book, perhaps indicating that the text is of lower resolution and thus quality than that on a page.

Computer-based learning text should contain more than the words. It should include the following:

- headings, subheadings and content (for example, words and illustrations)
- data about the nature of the subject (for example, sources, authors and websites)
- navigation clues showing the learners where they can go next or where they can access material from other parts of the package (for example, links, keywords and cross-references).

Instructions, messages and guidance

Similarly to other forms of open or distance learning material, computer-based learning presents a package which mainly relies on itself to convey understanding to the learner. In a classroom tutors can identify problems in comprehension and change their approach to overcome difficulties. A designer must be able to identify all the potential problems and build their solutions into the material. This is not just about the presentation of text on a screen. Many of the features, instructions and guidelines for using the materials are also conveyed in text.

All computer-based learning materials must:

- explain the nature of the learning material
- describe to the learners what they need to know and be able to do in order to study the package

Example
Learners should be competent computer users who are familiar with word processing, spreadsheets and databases in order to complete this module satisfactorily.

- explain what the learners will be able to do after studying the package, possibly in the form of a series of learning objectives (see Chapter 2)

Example
By the end of this section you will be able to:

a) define what constitutes human–computer interaction
b) describe what a user interface is

and so on

- provide learners with guidance on how to study the materials, such as how long it should take them, in what sequence to study the material and how to organize their learning. A study guide may be helpful either as a separate document or built into the computer package. If it is a document, it is often combined with installation instructions.

In face-to-face learning you can adapt your message to fit the situation whereas with computer-based learning you present all these messages and instructions on the computer screen. You must predict all the situations in advance without being able to see the impact your words make on the learners (for example, confusion). It is usual to test your material with an example of typical learners.

Communication approach

Learning materials should be presented in an informal friendly style to encourage learners to study. You can use a variety of styles:

- address the learner as 'you' and yourself (designer) as 'I' or 'we'
- use contractions such as 'we've', 'we'd', 'where's' and 'it's'
- write in plain English
- avoid jargon
- define new terms as they appear.

The overall aim is to produce material which the learners find easy to understand, as when designing an open learning workbook. The big difference derives from the nature of the medium. Computer-based learning is not suitable for the display of large quantities of text. Each display can show only a limited amount of information and it is best to restrict its content to a single idea, concept or chunk of information. The designer's aim is to provide a display which learners can easily comprehend, with links to related displays so that they understand the whole content.

Unlike writing for a book or magazine, you need to:

- break your text into meaningful chunks each presenting an individual idea
- link each chunk to other related ones so that each route is meaningful.

Example chunk

Rubber is a natural product. It is the sap of the rubber tree that has been vulcanized by heating it with sulphur. This process hardens and strengthens the sap to form commercial rubber. It is possible to synthesize rubber from oil.

Link from sap:

The sap is a white substance called latex. It is naturally sticky and rubbery. Rubber trees are found in tropical areas and have been harvested since the Stone Age. Modern rubber production is based on large plantations of rubber trees.

Chunking information is appropriate to all forms of computer-based learning materials but is particularly important to hypertext and online learning products. Books and other forms of paper-based writing are designed so that readers will start at the beginning and read to the end. In practice, readers often jump around the text, dipping in and out of the material using the contents list and index to allow them to concentrate on the areas which most interest them. Computer-based learning (including hypertext and online materials) is ideally suited to this form of reading. However, it does mean that you must write each chunk to stand alone and that learners should be able to study information chunks in a variety of orders. This is not easy to achieve. Here are some guidelines:

- Use cross-references to highlight related topics in order to encourage learners to study them.
- Provide a series of guided tours from different viewpoints.
- Allow learners to mark the route they take so that others can follow their paths.

Chunking is often linked to browsing, skimming or scanning where learners quickly browse the contents until they find material which meets their needs and then study it. However, browsing is a high level skill which is more likely to be used by confident learners with some experience of the subject. Novice learners who either lack confidence in themselves or are very new to the subject are likely to browse less and read more. This is important to take account of when designing the chunking strategy.

It is not easy to specify the size of a chunk of information. Common guidance is to aim for a chunk that fits on a single display, although subjects do not always break down into conveniently sized chunks so you may have to group a series of displays together. In this case you must clearly show learners that the frames are related. The simple device of numbering the pages or using linked headings is often effective (for example, page 1 of 4). When designing a chunk, calculate its size (number of words) and attempt to write each one to that standard. If you write on small cards you can experiment with the appearance of the information when it is read in a different order. However, do not force your subject to fit this size standard at the expense of the information. Many designers feel that some variation in the size of the chunk is good practice.

Scrolling

The computer display can scroll both horizontally and vertically (see Figure 5.2). Vertical scrolling moves the display up or down with the corresponding bottom or top lines and new line of text appearing. It can be confined in a window or fill the whole display.

Horizontal scrolling moves the display left or right and can be confined either to a single line of text or a whole page. In general users do not like scrolling text because it can disorientate them. If they are reading a long, vertically scrolling document they frequently get lost and find it difficult to locate the text they wish to refer back to. The best advice is simply not to scroll text, particularly if the learners are new computer users. If your learners are experienced then it is possible to employ vertical scrolling in a limited way.

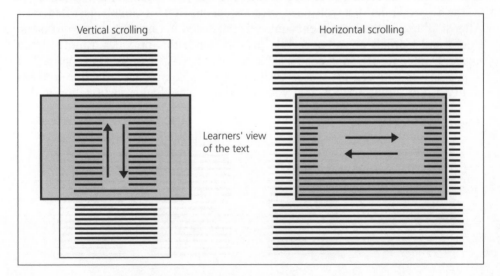

Figure 5.2   Horizontal and vertical scrolling

This compromise cannot be applied to horizontal scrolling which always results in only part of a line of text being visible. It is highly confusing, difficult to follow, and should not be used in learning materials.

Scrolling is particularly relevant to online learning materials where their appearance will be largely dependent on the learners' browsers. This can lead to a scrolling display which the designer did not intend. Always test online learning materials using different browsers and configurations to avoid the extremes of scrolling.

To summarize, the use of vertical scrolling should be limited to learners who are experienced computer users. Horizontal scrolling should be avoided.

Justification of text

There are four ways of justifying text – left, right, double and centred (see Figure 5.3). Left justified text is aligned parallel with the left margin of the screen or page and has a ragged right edge. Similarly, right justified text is aligned with the right margin and has a ragged left edge. Double justification presents text with both edges aligned in parallel with both margins. Centred text is aligned with the middle of the screen or page so that both edges are ragged.

As to which is best way of presenting text on the screen, the answer rests in considering the readability of the text and the experience of the readers. Right justified text is almost never used because it disrupts reading and should be avoided. The remaining three approaches are all used in books but centred text is normally only employed for titles or headings since it limits readability. It does, however, provide an effective way of drawing learners' attention to messages.

The two options that you need to consider are left or double justified text. Almost all text that a learner encounters is presented in one of these two formats. Books and journals are often double justified since this provides a professional image. Double justification can be achieved in a variety of ways. One approach is to add spaces between the words but this causes a significant reduction in read-ability. If the authoring tools that you are using create double justification in this

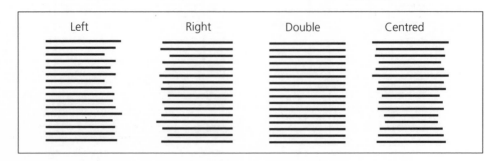

Figure 5.3   Justification

way, they should not be used – all text should be presented as left justified. Double justified text which is created by varying the space between individual letters does not seriously reduce readability. Left justified text is always readable so is the safe choice. You may occasionally wish to use text centred or double justified text to provide variety or to draw attention to certain parts of the display.

Text styles

Almost all text in books, newspapers, magazines, posters and informal writings is presented using both upper (for example, at the start of a sentence) and lower case. It is thus reasonable to follow this pattern when presenting text on a screen. The alternative approach is to use upper case alone (that is, capital letters). Although this has the benefit of emphasizing the message it is communicating, it also reduces readability, so is not suitable for long sections.

In addition to the choice of case there are other ways of emphasizing text:

- changing the font
- changing the character size
- using italics
- using bold
- underlining.

The computer offers a choice of many hundreds of fonts in a wide range of sizes, providing you with many combinations and opportunities to produce an interesting presentation in which you can emphasize key points. However, this almost limitless range of choices comes with the danger of distracting, disorienting and making the medium more important than the message. Good practice is to use a limited number of options with each combination of font and character size serving a distinct purpose.

Examples

Georgia – size 8

Times New Roman – size 12

Arial – size 16

Courier New – size 20

In a similar way, bold, italics and underlining provide additional options which enhance the presentation but also add complexity to your choices. Again, the risk is in using too many options. It is best to decide an overall style or approach for your material which minimizes the number of combinations and changes.

Example of style

Main headings	–	Arial size 16 bold
Subheadings	–	Arial size 14 bold
Body of text	–	Times New Roman size 12
Quotes	–	Times New Roman size 12 italics
Hypertext link	–	underlined
Questions	–	Arial size 12
Feedback	–	Arial size 12

Each combination should serve a precise purpose such as attention-getting, high-lighting information, making learners aware of the function of the text (for example, feedback) and enhancing readability. At the start of the project the design team should agree the styles to be used so that there is a consistent approach across the team and thus the design.

Newspaper techniques

Newspapers are designed to be easy to read. This is achieved by:

- effective use of white (blank space)
- dividing text into narrow columns (see Figures 5.4 and 5.5)
- using short plain English sentences.

It may seem that leaving blank or white space is irrelevant to the ease of reading of a piece of text. In fact, white space is a powerful means of drawing the learners' attention to the overall layout of your content, to headings and titles and to division of the display into chunks. This all adds considerable emphasis to the

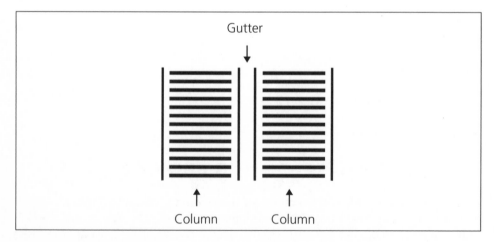

Figure 5.4   Columns of text

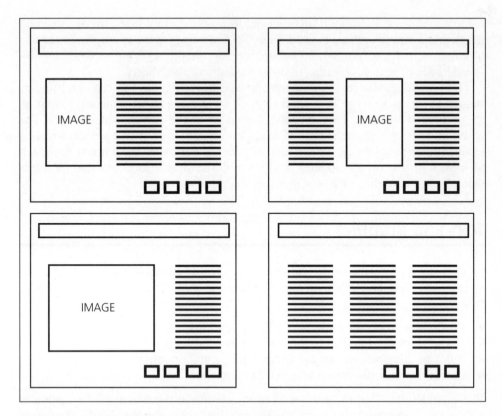

Figure 5.5   Examples of columns and screen displays

material. On the screen we are dealing with a medium that is not ideal for reading so white space is used to counter this negativity. It is good practice to double space computer-based learning text because the blank line helps the eye move quickly and efficiently from the end of one line to the beginning of the next, thus improving readability.

Let us consider how people read text. They fix their eyes on a word or small groups of words and then move to the next word or group. When the end of the line is reached they must move to the start of the next line. The speed of reading is the number of fixations multiplied by the length of each one plus the time taken to move to a new line. Readability is likely to be best when this process works smoothly and without difficulty. The more the reader has to return to earlier words or groups of words to understand the text or to find the next line, the lower the readability of the material.

The longer the line of text, the more difficult it is to locate the start of the next line. Double spacing will help solve this problem but a more powerful aid is to divide the text into narrow columns. This also aids readability by allowing readers to scan whole lines of words easily. Newspapers do not normally double space a column but it is useful to do so on a screen. Newspapers also employ multiple columns while on the screen it is unusual to produce more than two or three and frequently a single column is used. Figure 5.5 provides some examples of the use of columns and illustrations. To summarize, divide the screen into short double-spaced lines of text or columns in order to improve readability.

The normal guidance for producing straightforward, easy-to-read and under-standable text is to write in a plain English style using short sentences – that is, about 10 to 12 words. This appears to transfer to the screen equally well. The width of a screen column is limited to approximately four or five words, which is again similar to a newspaper column. If you are not using a columnar approach then lines of text on a computer screen should be short. Good practice indicates that a length of eight to ten words is the optimum.

Text and graphics

Pictures are a powerful aid to learning and are most effective when related to the surrounding text and other media. The general guidelines for their use are as follows:

- Illustrations relevant to the text will aid learning.
- Illustrations not relevant to the text will not aid learning.
- Relevant illustrations can aid understanding and retention of the text.
- Learners prefer illustrated text to text on its own.

These guidelines need to be considered in relation to the nature of the computer screen and computer-based learning. The medium is not suitable for the display of large amounts of text so it must be broken into meaningful chunks, thus suggest-

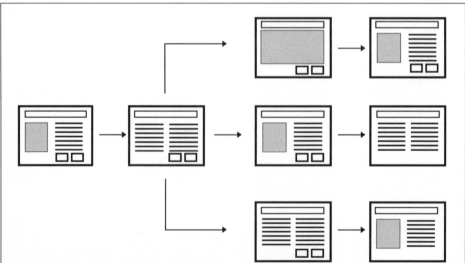

Figure 5.6   Illustrations and text combinations

ing that relevant illustrations will be very suitable since they can convey large quantities of information. A chunk now becomes more than just text. It can be a relevant picture with text, or alternating text and picture frames. The most effective chunk will probably be a mixture of a picture and text, but linking a text chunk to a picture chunk may also be effective. The important factor is that the picture must be closely linked to the text. It is probably reasonable to alternate text and picture frames but separating the picture from the text by more than a single frame will reduce the effect of the picture. A series of illustrations followed or proceeded by text is unlikely to be totally effective. Figure 5.6 demonstrates the possible combinations of picture, picture-only and text and text-only displays. All illustrations should be as memorable as possible to assist learners in recalling the content.

Structured text

Structured text is a type of illustration. The position of the text on the screen provides additional information as does the grouping of information. It is very useful in a medium which does not support long passages of text and in which learners find reading uncomfortable because it can communicate considerable information in a concise manner. A table is a structured display in that the rows and columns show the interrelationship of the different items and group related information. The following example shows a structured display.

Example
To write an overview of the elements which make up the world we live in would require many pages of text and would be difficult to understand. The relationships between elements would be hard to follow and to remember. If you attempted this type of overview using computer-based learning material you would require scores of frames or pages of text. Mendeleev, a Russian scientist, designed a structured display which summarizes the relationships between all the elements on a single page. This is called the periodic table. A portion of the table is shown in Figure 5.7.

An understanding of the structure of the periodic table is vital to accessing the rich information it contains and this is also true of any structured display. The periodic table is arranged in order of atomic number with each cell showing the element symbol, relative atomic mass and atomic number.

Example
H – element symbol (hydrogen)
1 – relative atomic mass
1 – atomic number

Each column consists of a group of elements which react similarly to each other although there are changes as you move down the column (see, for example, the alkali metals in the left-hand vertical column of Figure 5.7).

H 1 1			
Li 7 3	Be 9 4		
Na 23 11	Mg 24 12		
K 39 19	Ca 40 20	Sc 45 21	Ti 48 22
Rb 85 37	Sr 88 38	Y 89 39	Ze 91 40
Ca 133 55	Ba 137 56	La 139 57	Hf 178 72
Fr 223 87	Ra 226 88	Ac 227 89	Ku 260 104

Figure 5.7   Periodic table

Learners need to understand the structure in order to extract the information presented to them. If they do not understand the structure it will not assist learning and may, in fact, hinder it. It is good practice to provide an explanation of structure and follow the approach consistently throughout the material.

The main guidelines for structuring text are:

- Display key information prominently.
- Group related information together.
- Provide a fixed format so learners understand the layout.
- Use a concise display of text.

Structured text can convey a large amount of information in a small display space. It is therefore a useful approach in computer-based learning, a medium not ideal for the presentation of text. However, you must help learners to understand the structure or it will simply be an interesting abstract illustration.

Text and colour

Colour is a powerful motivating force. Learners often judge coloured material as being of better quality than black and white. By using a range of coloured texts, it is possible to highlight different messages and provide your learners with a learning map. However, fundamental issues are readability and legibility. The foreground and background colours are the key to legibility. In your choice of colours, you need to maximize contrast. Some effective choices are:

Foreground	*Background*
Yellow	Black
White	Black
Cyan	Black
Black	Yellow
White	Blue
Blue	Cyan

Choice of colour is not simply about maximizing legibility. Colours have significant cultural meaning for many people (for example, red = danger) so care must be taken not to select inappropriate ones. Individuals often have preferences for certain colours which may influence their reaction to them. It is very difficult to allow for individual or group preferences, so testing of your colour selection is critical to its successful employment.

Reversing contrast (for example, displaying white text on a black background) is the opposite of normal practice (see Figure 5.8), and is thus an effective way of highlighting information. However, like other attention focusing devices, if it is over-used it is likely to become ineffective or even negative.

This is an example of reversing the conventional display of black text on a white background – that is, a white foreground and a black background. It is intended to draw learners' attention to the text more effectively than the normal display.

Figure 5.8   Reverse contrast

Highlighting

Highlighting key parts of a text display you can ensure that the learners' attention is attracted to important information. Attention is drawn to features such as headings, cross-references and hypertext links. Online documents on the World Wide Web often employ underlining to indicate that the word is a hypertext link. The underlining changes colour (for example, red to blue) when it has been used. This simple device is very useful to a learner.

Highlighting devices which can be used on text displays include:

- changing character size (for example, larger size for headings)
- capitals
- bold, italics and underlining (for example, italics to indicate a quote)
- colour
- reverse video
- flashing (for example, warning messages)
- boxing – enclosing a message in a rectangle
- combinations of several methods.

Remember to establish a pattern of highlighting which is linked to the importance of the information.

Example

Main headings	Capitals, bold, size 20
Subheadings	Bold, size 14
Warning messages	Flashing heading, red, size 14
Hypertext link	Red underline which turns blue after link has been accessed
Feedback	Boxed

Summaries, reviews, overviews and reminders

The nature of computer-based learning text is that it is broken up into relatively small chunks of information which learners may study in a variety of orders. It is therefore important to include summaries of the material so that learners are given a second opportunity to understand the key points. For similar reasons it is important to provide regular reviews of the content as well as overviews to help learners decide if they want to study particular sections. Paper-based open learning uses lists as an effective way of reminding learners of what they have studied. In computer-based learning checklists are also useful.

Short summaries, reviews of material, overviews of content and reminders (for example, checklists) of what has been studied are very useful in this context. They will aid the learners' choice of routes and refresh their understanding of the content. Learning is helped by repetition so long as it is presented effectively and interestingly. Good learning design can be considered as an attempt to write the same messages in a variety of interesting, motivating and easy to understand forms and presentations.

Summary of key points

Presentation

- The quality of text on the screen is significantly poorer than print on a page.
- Learners do not find reading text on a screen easy or pleasant.
- Learners read text more slowly on the screen than on the page.
- Computer-based learning text holds headings, content, sources and navigation clues.
- Designers must identify potential problems which learners may encounter and build solutions into the design.

Communication approach

- Explain what learners will be able to do after studying the package.
- Present learning materials in an informal friendly way.
- Divide text into chunks so that learners comprehend each chunk and the whole content no matter which route they take.

Scrolling

- Use vertical scrolling in a limited way only with computer literate learners. Do not use with new computer users. Horizontal scrolling should not be used at all in learning materials.

Justification

- Text should usually be left or double justified. However, avoid double justification if it is achieved by adding spaces between words – readability will be reduced.

Text styles

- Use of too many of the choices of font, size, italics, bold, underlining and colour can be distracting and confusing.
- Agree a style for the package.

Newspaper techniques

- Newspaper techniques improve readability of computer-based learning (for example, white space, dividing text into columns and writing short sentences).

Text and graphics

- Illustrations should be relevant to the text to aid learning.
- Illustrations should not be separated too far from the relevant text.

Structured text

- Structured text is an efficient way of presenting information.

Text and colour

- Colour is a powerful motivating force.
- Maximize contrast between foreground and background colours to ensure readability.

Highlighting

- Establish a clear pattern for the use of highlighting devices. Too many different approaches will confuse and distract learners.

Summaries reviews and checklists

- Use summaries, reviews and checklists to ensure overall comprehension of computer-based learning material.

Chapter 6

Use of colour

By the end of this chapter you will have been introduced to:

- what is colour?
- colour and learning
- systematic use of colour
- highlighting
- number of colours
- coloured text
- colour preferences
- colour combinations
- colour and graphics.

Several examples of the use of colour have been provided on the Gower website at http://www.gowerpub.com which illustrate some of the ideas discussed in this chapter.

What is colour?

The human eye can recognize millions of colours or, rather, shades of colours. Computers are capable of producing these shades by mixing three colours – red, blue and green. Three variables are used to describe colour:

- hue
- saturation, and
- intensity.

Hue is what we normally call colour – for example red, blue and green. Saturation is a way of describing the purity of a colour and how it varies from grey to its most pure vivid form. Intensity is a measure of the lightness (or darkness) of a colour. The colour shade you see is a combination of hue, saturation and intensity, with the result that there are many shades of red, blue and green.

How can colour enhance the design of learning materials?

Colour is a powerful motivating force. People will often judge coloured products as having a higher value and quality than the equivalent monochrome products. It is an important way of gaining learners' attention, reinforcing key points and segregating information.

Some degree of colour blindness affects about 8 per cent of people in the Western world, the main problem being that they cannot distinguish between red and green. If you displayed red text on a green background it would be invisible to some colour blind people. In the main, more men suffer from colour blindness than women so this is an important factor if your learners are predominantly male. It is sensible to use colour as an additional cue or focusing device combined with other design elements such as graphical features (for example, lines and boxes). The learners are therefore provided with two opportunities to have their attention drawn to the key information or to realize that certain chunks of information are related. You should test the interface on a monochrome display to ensure that colour blind individuals are not disadvantaged by the design.

Colour can serve a wide variety of roles including:

- attracting learners' attention
- aiding retention of learning
- emphasizing key points or areas of the display
- adding interest to a display or illustration
- helping learners to identify an individual object in a complex display (for example, simulation of a process plant)
- grouping objects and information together.

To gain the positive advantages of using colour it must be used in a systematic way to achieve a distinct objective. Random use of colour because it appears attractive is not going to achieve your goals. It is likely to have the opposite effect. It can add to eye strain and may cause after-images to appear to learners for some time after they have completed using the material. Colour provides visual clues to attract the learner but needs to be used consistently and systematically. You must decide what you want to draw the learners' attention to. Colour can be a distraction if over-used.

Colours are often associated with particular meanings such as:

- red for danger
- black for mourning
- purple for regal
- yellow for excitement
- violet for mysterious
- green for placid.

However, meaning changes according to the cultural background of the learners and even within one cultural group it can vary. This makes selecting colours for a particular application difficult unless you test your selections on your target audience. There is no substitute for testing.

Systematic versus random use of colour

Few people would buy a random range of tins of paint and simply paint their walls with the first one which came to hand expecting to produce anything attractive. Similarly, to produce computer-based learning materials by, for example, tossing a coin for which colours to use and how to use them will not aid learning. It is more likely to result in a package which confuses, distracts, makes the learners' attitudes to the material negative and hinders the learning process. No designer would intentionally use colour in this way but it can be the outcome if you underestimate the power of colour for aiding and hindering learning.

When you are planning your package, you must consider the role which colour will play in the material.

- Be consistent in your use of colour (for example, all feedback messages will use the same colours).
- Limit the number of colours.
- Be clear about the role colour is playing (for example, drawing the learners' attention to key information).
- Use colour to add extra visual clues to the interface and avoid disadvantaging colour blind learners.

Colour is like a code that learners must appreciate in order to understand the interface. When they know that blue always indicates a heading they can understand the interface. Otherwise it is just an attractive colour to brighten the display. Learners gain a knowledge of the code from using the material. If colour is used consistently they can perceive the patterns. The perception of the patterns can be aided by using colour to enhance other visual features such as graphical objects (for example, lines and boxes). However, when too many colours are used for too many purposes the task of understanding the code is made more difficult and learners can become overwhelmed by the display – like identifying a individual tree in a forest of similar trees.

At the start of a project it is useful to decide on your approach by defining the use of different colours such as:

Main headings	Red/grey	size 16 bold
Subheadings	Red/grey	size 14
Background colour	Cyan	
Foreground colour	Dark blue	size 12
Key information	Black/cyan	size 12
Feedback	Red/yellow	size 12
Questions	Magenta/yellow	size 12

By planning your application of colour in a systematic way you will gain the greatest effect.

Highlighting

Colour may be used to highlight information or areas of the display. It is very effective in drawing the attention of learners. However, there are limits and guidelines to ensure that it is used efficiently. Learners must understand the role that a particular colour is playing (for example, feedback always has a yellow background, errors use red text and magenta highlights a key point). If they do not understand the code then the ability of colour to highlight information is substantially reduced. In designing computer-based learning you need to help the learner to develop this knowledge. Many packages provide a short introduction to the workings of the materials so you can use this to introduce learners to the use of colour.

Colour helps learners to locate information on a display but its effect can be seriously reduced if the screen is overcrowded with information and images. The more crowded the display the less effective colour will be. However, a complex monochrome display can be aided by using some colour since this will provide a breakdown of the complexity into discrete areas. On http://www.gowerpub.com Figure 6.1 demonstrates the use of a limited range of highlighting. The illustration shows a coloured title bar and control buttons. The colour has been used to emphasize these features and learners will find them easier to locate.

The highlighting effect of colour can be enhanced if it is combined with basic graphics such as enclosing an area in a box or underlining. The two devices work together to emphasize areas of the display and capture the learners' attention. This is very useful in computer-based learning where you will often need to divide a screen display into distinct areas by their purpose, such as questions, options and feedback. On http://www.gowerpub.com Figure 6.2 provides a simple example of a question and answer display using graphics and colour. Colour has been combined with the simple graphical feature of a rectangle.

It is difficult to say which is the more powerful highlighting device, colour or graphics, but it is clear that combining them is particularly effective. The limiting factor is that overuse of colour is likely to make identifying and distinguishing between highlighted elements more difficult.

Other ways of highlighting information include:

- inverse video, and
- blinking.

Inverse video means reversing the colours in contrast to the rest of the display (for example, black becomes white and white turns into black). The item thus stands out from the rest of the display and the learners' attention is drawn to it. Blinking is where the item flashes on and off rather like a lighthouse. Both devices provide alternatives to colour but colour is probably more effective.

Information may also be highlighted by changing character size, underlining, colour, inverse video and using different fonts. Remember to use highlighting in a consistent way so that learners understand its importance and don't become confused and distracted by too many different methods being used. It is good practice to use highlighting methods consistently throughout the package and to limit the number of techniques on any one screen display and throughout the material.

Number of colours

Designers are often advised to limit the number of colours they employ when designing computer-based learning materials. However, this is seldom quantified or explained. The complicating factor is that other structural devices may be combined with colour which make the display more complex and difficult to resolve. If colour is used as the only attention-seeking device, then more can be used. If it is combined with graphics, different fonts and character size then less should be employed.

All this makes deciding how many colours to use very difficult. A simple answer is only to use colour for distinct purposes which relate to the learning objectives. This means that there are few occasions when you need to use more than five or six colours and seven is probably a maximum. If you intend to use more than seven you should critically analyse your reasons.

The addition of even a modest amount of colour is likely to add interest. A coloured background may have a significant effect on motivating the learners by making them feel that it is a worthwhile product to study. It will not overcome the learners' reaction to poor learning material but it will contribute to providing the initial impetus with other factors to encourage them to consider the package. The overuse of colour is likely to have the opposite effect in that learners may be unwilling to concentrate on the material because it distracts and confuses them.

Most of this discussion has assumed that the material consists largely of text and graphical images which are likely to result in a straightforward relatively uncomplicated display. Some forms of computer-based learning are more complex and can be simplified by using a larger than average number of colours. Simulations are often visually complex and colour can assist learners to understand them. On http:// www.gowerpub.com Figure 6.3 shows a simulation of a process plant control desk with many output dials, indicators, alarms, buttons and controls. The colour provides a means of grouping similar controls and helping the learner understand how they relate together. This use of colour to group objects together is a very useful highlighting role because helping learners to see relationships between objects, ideas and issues is part of a wide range of subjects.

Coloured text

Most text which learners encounter is black on a white background. Computers can provide a wide range of colours for both text and background and thus produce a multicoloured display. However, this is unlikely to aid learning. It is more likely to distract, tire, cause eye strain and irritate your learners. Colour must be used in a systematic purposeful way. The first essential is that the text is easy to read which means that the contrast between the coloured text and the background needs to be high. This is the key to text which your learners can clearly discern and read. On http://www.gowerpub.com Figure 6.4 shows a range of examples of different coloured text and different backgrounds.

The classic combination of black text on a white background should not be dismissed simply because it is well established and seemingly conservative. It has excellent legibility although it obviously does not take advantage of the computer's ability to display a range of colours. Uses of coloured text include:

- hypertext links (for example, live links are red and change to blue when activated)
- glossary entries (for example, by clicking on blue words their definition appears)
- headings and subheadings
- identifying questions, exercises and activities
- extra notes
- labelling diagrams and other illustrations
- button titles
- help messages.

Colour preferences

It is clear that individuals have colour preferences that may well affect their behaviour. The problem for the designer is to identify the preferences of the group with whom they are working. Many commercial computer applications (for example, operating systems) provide users with the option to customize the colours used by the system. If you walk across an open plan office and observe the different displays it is clear that users like to customize their displays to suit their preferences. A wide range of colours will be visible showing the individual preferences of the users.

When designing computer-based learning you can obviously allow learners to select their preferred colours. An operating system user will be working on the computer for many hours over a period of months or even years so the extra burden of selecting colours is very small, whereas a learner may only use the learning material once. Do you want to add the burden of choosing colours which may demotivate the learners from studying the package? A good general principle is to reduce the load on the learners so they can concentrate on the material and not the computer system. However, if the learners hate your selected colours, it is not going to encourage them to study the material. This is a genuine dilemma. A possible solution is simply to test your choices with a sample of typical learners, which should avoid the main problems of colour selection.

Colour combinations

There is a wide range of foreground and background colours which can be used effectively in computer-based learning. The colour spectrum provides a guide to selecting colours:

> Violet   Blue   Cyan   Green   Yellow   Orange   Red

Adjacent colours offer good contrast (light and dark to each other) and thus aid readability. Colours on the extreme edges of the spectrum and which are fully saturated should be avoided since they often irritate the eye.

Some suggestions for colour combinations are listed in Table 6.1 but there is no

Table 6.1   *Colour combinations*

Background colour	Foreground (text) colours
Grey	Cyan
	White
	Yellow
Dark blue	Cyan
	White
	Yellow
Yellow	Magenta
	Black
	Blue
Cyan	Black
	Yellow
	White
Black	Cyan
	Green
	Yellow
	White
Green	Magenta
	White
Red	Cyan
	Green
Magenta	Black
	Yellow
White	Black
	Blue

substitute for testing choices with typical learners and viewing the material on the chosen monitors. Different monitors and computers will present colours in different ways. Materials which are shown by a video projector on a large screen will appear differently on a computer screen. You must test your computer-based learning materials in the environment in which they will be used.

Table 6.1 gives a selection of background colours with a number of choices for the foreground. A dark background colour is gentler on the learners' eyes so black, dark blue and dark grey are good choices. They convey a relaxed atmosphere to learners which may help reduce the stress on them. They are probably most effective if learners are studying a display over a long period of time, but good practice is to divide material into short chunks of learning and thus avoid the need for lengthy periods of concentration. Dark colours tend to be identified in some cultures with sadness and normally you do not want to depress your learners. Motivation to learn should be linked to excitement, interest and stimulation. A dark background should perhaps be used only occasionally to provide a clear contrast with the rest of the material. You could reverse the background from white/light grey to black/dark grey when you are asking learners to take part in an assessment exercise. The change would alert them that they are undertaking a different task and emphasize the importance of the assessment. On http://www.gowerpub.com Figure 6.5 shows this reverse contrast approach.

Colour and graphics

We live in a coloured world, so it is natural to provide coloured illustrations. The computer can produce realistic coloured photographs or employ colour to emphasize data on a graph, chart or table. Colour can add value to all types of illustration by drawing attention to the key points. However, it can be over-used. If you are presenting a table of data and want to highlight the differences between the rows you could colour each row differently. This would produce an interesting display but how are learners to identify what are the differences since everything is coloured? In contrast you could highlight a row if the learners select it by reversing the colours. This would help learners to focus on that particular row and avoid confusing it with the others. On http://www.gowerpub.com Figure 6.6 demonstrates this technique.

Pie charts, histograms and bar charts employ shape and size to present numerical information in a way that it is straightforward to compare and contrast. On http://www.gowerpub.com Figure 6.7 provides an illustration of combining colour with these charts. Colour offers an additional mechanism to code the data and increases learners' understanding of the information. These types of graphic are very efficient in presenting complex information which would normally require a large volume of text to explain. However, they do require learners to perceive the differences between the numerical data. Colour can aid this differentiation.

Colour shading can be employed effectively to show depth or height. By slowly changing the shade of an individual colour you can illustrate a mountain or the depth of a pond or lake (see Figure 6.8 at http://www.gowerpub.com).

Summary of key points

General issues

- Colour is made up of three variables – hue, saturation and intensity.
- Learners are motivated by colour.
- Colour blindness affects about 8 per cent of people in the Western world. More men suffer from colour blindness than women.
- Individual colours have meanings (for example, white for purity) but these vary between and within different cultures.

Good practice

- Use colour consistently and systematically.
- Do not use too many colours (that is, no more than 5 to 7).
- Use colour to add extra visual clues to the interface (for example, in addition to graphical features).
- Colour is very effective in highlighting information and areas of the display.
- Colour is one of a range of different highlighting techniques (for example, inverse video) which need to be used consistently.
- Colour can group objects together, so learners are able to identify relationships between objects, ideas and issues.
- Coloured text must be legible. Maximize the contrast between the coloured text and the background.
- Graphics of all types can be enhanced by the use of colour.

Testing

- To ensure the selection of colours is suitable, always test your material with a sample of typical learners, using a range of hardware and in the learning environment.

Chapter 7

Use of graphics

By the end of this chapter you will have been introduced to:

- graphics and learning
- types of illustration
- relating text to images
- structural or graphical organizers
- design of icons and buttons
- combining colour and graphics
- descriptive and instructional captions
- icons and buttons
- lines, borders and frames
- multiple images.

How can illustrations aid learning and retention?

Illustrations are recognized as having the potential to aid learning. In all forms of education and training, a single picture can convey a large amount of information. The computer screen is not an ideal environment to present text because of the reduced resolution compared to print on paper, so pictures have an extra potential advantage in computer-based learning.

Illustrations in computer-based learning can take many forms including:

- photographs
- full and part screen images
- graphics
- geometrical
- cartoons
- line drawings

- charts and graphs
- analogies
- icons.

All the above could be presented in colour or monochrome.

The guidelines for using all these forms of illustrations to aid learning include:

1. Illustrations must be relevant to the content of the learning material.
2. Images can substitute for words.
3. Learners may not perceive the full information content of an illustration.
4. Learners prefer illustrated material.
5. Images are particularly helpful to learners with poor reading skills.

The most important guideline is to integrate the images into the material. The text should link to the illustration and the pictures should support the text or other media. This mutual support is vital to assisting learning. Using images simply as attractive wallpaper will not enhance learning.

Types of illustration

Illustrations can be divided into three types in terms of assisting the learning process (Alesandrini, 1987). These are:

- representational/realistic
- analogical
- logical.

This classification is based on their role in learning.

Representational illustrations are those which share a physical resemblance to the object or concept they are portraying. A photograph is a realistic image.

Analogical images illustrate a topic or a concept by implying a similarity (for example, showing a picture of a cheetah as an analogy for speed). It is vital that learners are able to comprehend the analogy. An analogue illustration should help users to interpret new information in the light of prior knowledge and thus assist the learning process.

Logical graphics do not resemble the physical things they represent but are a logical representation of them. Examples of this type of graphic are flow charts, graphs and charts.

Representational/realistic illustrations

Realistic images are probably what most people see as 'pictures' in that they look like the real object. The degree of resemblance may vary from a photograph to an outline drawing of the object and includes cartoons and other graphic images.

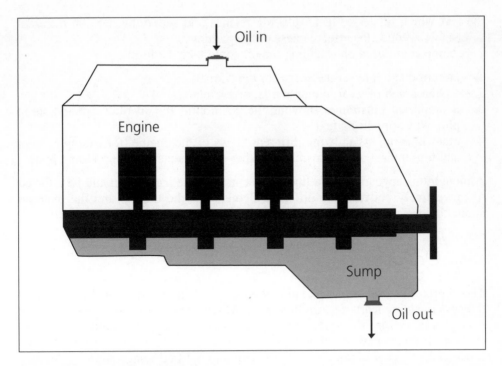

Figure 7.1   Instructional illustration

Photographs and other highly realistic pictures are often powerful motivational forces in making subjects interesting. They are important in putting the subject in its correct context. To explain to learners how to change the oil in a car without a picture is both difficult and also likely to mislead. The topic is visual and a picture of a car will gain interest while illustrations of the sump and oil cap are essential to locate the correct parts. However, a photograph will not show you the internal workings of the engine and so would not help learners to understand where the oil goes. To provide this detail requires a drawing showing what oil does when it is poured into the engine. This type of illustration is not particularly motivating but is nevertheless essential for instructing learners in the working of the engine.

Figure 7.1 shows a cross-section of a car engine with the oil filler cap and sump illustrated. This would help learners to understand the role that oil plays in the engine but would be enhanced by text explaining that the oil is pumped around the engine and that the illustration does not show the oil pump or filter which are other important components of the system. Labelling the picture is also important because it will draw the learners' attention to key parts of the engine.

Realistic illustrations essentially provide information and motivation. However, they are not independent of other types of information and to gain maximum benefit they should be closely related to the text. Computer-based learning material provides a relatively small area to display information (that is, a single or multiple screen display), so ideally an image should appear on the same screen as the text which relates to it. Displaying images and supporting text on different screens will reduce the effectiveness of the pictures.

A complete tutorial on changing the oil could take the form of:

1. an introduction to set the scene for the learners
2. a photograph of a car to gain the learner's interest
3. a simplified illustration showing the position of the oil filler cap and sump plug with supporting text
4. other illustrations showing different views of the engine (for example, front and top) indicating the position of other components, with supporting text.

Although this appears to be a linear presentation, the learners should be allowed to move freely between the different elements of the tutorial and the material should be designed to maximize interactivity.

Degree of detail

The degree of detail that a picture shows is proportionately related to its effectiveness in aiding learning. An illustration which shows all the detail of an image may gain the learners' attention but make it difficult for them to identify the key elements from the mass of other detail. This obviously depends on the object being illustrated. A general guide is to start with a simplified image showing the key parts you would like the learners to concentrate on and then gradually build up the detail so that learners are systematically taken through the different elements. Complete this sequence by using a photograph to show the actual object. However, if you are seeking to interest learners, an initial photograph is more likely to succeed than a simple line drawing.

Figure 7.2 shows three views of an axle and a wheel, each differing in the degree of detail they reveal. The first illustration simply shows that the axle and wheel are joined, the second shows the bolts and nuts used to make the link, and the third image reveals the suspension. Each could serve a distinct learning purpose:

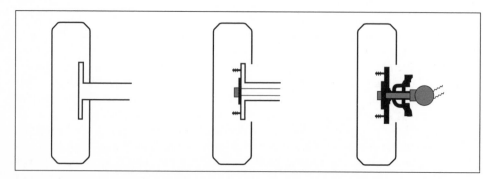

Figure 7.2   Axle and wheel

- image 1 – as part of an introduction for new probationary drivers
- image 2 – as part of a tutorial for changing a wheel
- image 3 – as part of a tutorial on car maintenance.

The purpose of illustrations is closely related to the degree of detail shown. An actual picture of an object is often the best form of motivation but disguises the important features either beneath its surface or within the detail of the image. A simplified image allows the main features of the object to be identified, while a picture showing the internal workings or features can be very helpful to learners.

Analogical illustrations

An analogical image illustrates a concept so that through knowledge of an object you gain an insight into the concept. Figure 7.3 shows an image of a butterfly. This could be used to suggest the concept of fragility which you cannot illustrate directly. However, it is only effective if the learners have experience of butterflies and know they are extremely fragile creatures. Fragility could also be illustrated using a glass. The image you select should be based on what the learners will recognize.

Analogies provide the learners with a way of making a link to their previous experience and knowledge. They consider the new material in contrast with their existing understanding. This is a powerful way of aiding learning if the learners can recognize the relationship between the analogical illustration and their previous experience. However, if they fail to perceive the link then at best the picture may seem out of place or at worst they will believe it is a representational image and will try to fit it into the tutorial. It is potentially very confusing.

To describe knowledge of a subject as similar to a fishing net is to suggest to learners that there are many gaps (that is, holes in the net) in our understanding of the subject but that it does have a structure (the strands of the net). This image provides a useful mental picture to learners. However, if they do not make the

Figure 7.3   Fragility

connection between knowledge of the subject and the physical structure of the net then they may well be more confused than if the analogy was not used. It is therefore important to support the illustration with text so that this risk is minimized.

Designers commonly use analogical images to illustrate the whole learning package to help users understand its overall structure. This type of illustration, if understood, will help learners make better use of all the resources contained in the system. A wide variety of analogies have been used including geographical maps, room plans and different types of books.

Logical illustrations

There is a wide range of logical illustrations such as: histograms, pie charts, time series graphs, tables of information and bar charts. They all offer ways of presenting a large volume of information to help learners compare different elements with each other and appreciate different quantities. However, logical images do require learners to understand their nature in order to understand the information being presented. If learners are not aware that the height of each element of a histogram (see Figure 7.4) represents its respective size, then it can be meaningless (that is, merely an odd shaped image).

All logical illustrations require learners to have an understanding of the image:

- graphs – understanding of axes, scales and gradients
- pie charts – understanding that size is represented proportionately by each slice
- tables – understanding of the relationship between rows and columns.

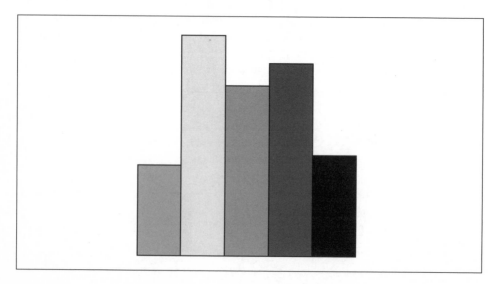

Figure 7.4   Logical graphic

Table A		Table B	
AAAAA	AAAAA	AAAAA	AAAAA
AAAAA	AAAAA	AAAAA	AAAAA
AAAAA	AAAAA	AAAAA	AAAAA
AAAAA	AAAAA	AAAAA	AAAAA
		AAAAA	AAAAA
AAAAA	AAAAA	AAAAA	AAAAA
AAAAA	AAAAA	AAAAA	AAAAA
AAAAA	AAAAA	AAAAA	AAAAA
AAAAA	AAAAA	AAAAA	AAAAA
		AAAAA	AAAAA
AAAAA	AAAAA	AAAAA	AAAAA
AAAAA	AAAAA	AAAAA	AAAAA
AAAAA	AAAAA	AAAAA	AAAAA
AAAAA	AAAAA	AAAAA	AAAAA

Figure 7.5   Separating chunks of information

The computer screen does not provide a large display area so logical images have the potential to present a lot of information to learners. They are particularly useful in demonstrating trends and relationships. Logical graphics are rich in information but they must be studied in order to gain access to the knowledge they contain. Few can be deciphered in a single glance. More often, they need to be systematically analysed.

Tables can display very dense amounts of information which can be difficult to extract. A table of numerical information will not be understood in a few moments. It requires careful analysis. Designers can help learners to identify information effectively by grouping it into related chunks, possibly by leaving blank lines between chunks of data. In Figure 7.5 table A will be easier to study and understand than table B since it is broken into smaller chunks. Other ways of grouping information include:

- colour coding the different chunks of information. This should be done with care since it is easy to use too many colours and hinder selection of the different parts. Colour is nevertheless a powerful means of identifying elements in a complex display
- using solid lines to separate information
- employing different fonts and character sizes. However, this should not be over-used as it may confuse and distract.

It is good practice to provide an exercise within the tutorial to ensure that learners spend adequate time considering the content of the logical image. Without this integration many images will be only partially effective. Integrating logical graphics with other content will add to their value. A simulation of a car accelerating could be combined with a table showing the distance travelled at different speeds.

This would help learners see the relationship between speed and distance in two different ways.

Structural or graphical organizers

Organizers are schematic representations of the relationship between concepts. They highlight the key points and activate the users' relevant prior knowledge. An organizer could be a map of a website showing the relationship between the different elements which make up the site. One of the best known graphical organizers is the London Underground map which shows the relationship between the different lines and the position of each station. It helps users to understand quickly which lines they need to travel to any destination. This is achieved by simplifying the actual map of the different lines, providing a distinctive colour code and concentrating on the relationships between the different elements. Whilst often difficult to design, graphic organizers can be highly effective in aiding the understanding of a complex subject. Figure 7.6 illustrates an organizer in the form of a task analysis for changing a car's oil.

Practice has shown that if learners use a structured computer display which explains the nature of the learning material prior to encountering the actual system the result is often:

● less mistakes in navigation
● more effective use of the material.

Users are provided with a framework which assists organization of the task and association of subsequent information which must be understood. However, it

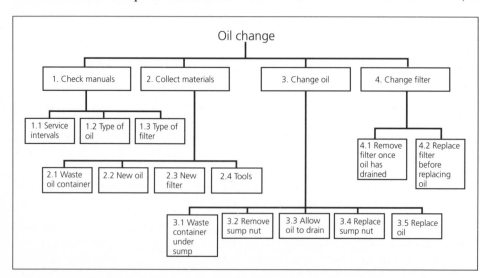

Figure 7.6   Organizer

does assume that learners are willing and able to study and comprehend the organizer. In some cases learners are anxious to make progress and see the organizer as something to get through quickly. In other cases learners do not make the link between the organizer and the learning material. This is similar to the problem learners have with recognizing an analogy.

Multiple illustrations

The computer screen can display images of different types, sizes and shapes either as multiple images or a single image filling the whole display. From a designer's point of view consider what you are aiming to achieve with the display and how you intend to explain its purpose to your learners. Learners confronted with many different illustrations will find their attention split, each separate image being too small to see a great deal of detail. If you wish to provide learners with many examples then you are probably limited to simple identification since the details will be lost. Figure 7.7 shows a display of 12 illustrations which appears to be symmetrical and even attractive but each image is only about one inch square thus limiting the detail it can show. It is possible to design the display so that by clicking on an image, it grows to a sufficient size to see the details. Figure 7.8 shows an example of this technique where a one-inch square image is increased to approximately nine square inches. Many static small images can be displayed in this way or a continuous cycle of images can be rotated through the screen. This technique can provide many options to learners but it is likely that only a selection of illustrations will be considered in depth. Few learners will explore all the options.

An alternative to this type of multiple illustration display is a slide show (see Figure 7.9). The different illustrations are shown one at a time. The images can be related together to form a presentation (for example, showing how to repair a machine) or can be different examples of an object or any other combination

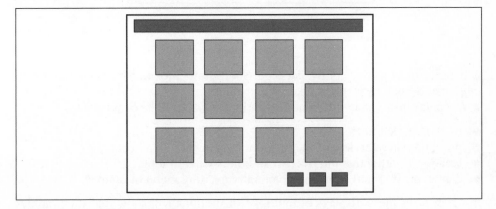

Figure 7.7   **Multiple illustrations**

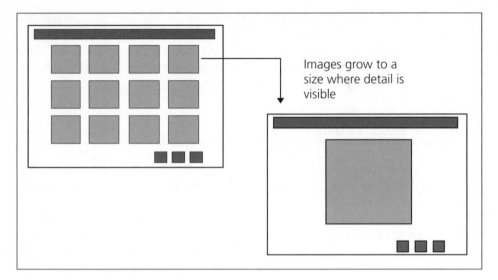

Figure 7.8   Growing an image

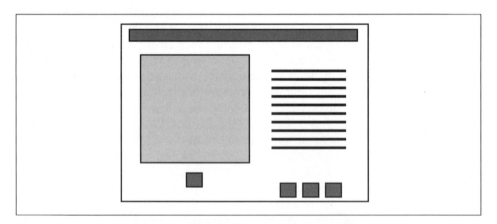

Figure 7.9   Slide show

which fits the objectives of the package. Slide shows are often best combined with other media such as text or spoken commentary.

A display with many different illustrations is likely to be best for:

- motivating learners
- providing an overview of the material by showing many examples
- creating an attractive interface to an otherwise dull topic
- displaying an interesting and potentially exciting menu of options.

In many cases these displays of multiple illustrations will show realistic graphics and pictures. It is perfectly possible to show many different logical (charts, graphs and tables) or multiple analogical images, but what would be the purpose of many different analogies on a single display? Would learners be able to recognize them all as analogies and make the links to their previous experiences? It is doubtful if anything would be achieved except that learners would be confused by the display and either ignore it or give it an unpredictable meaning.

In contrast, multiple logical images can provide a large learning resource. Learners could be given exercises which require them to study the different charts, graphs and tables in order to carry out the activities. Without this form of integration, it is doubtful if learners would consider each image in sufficient detail to gain even a fraction of the information available. Mixing a range of images (for example, real photographs, analogies, charts and tables) is technically possible, but while it would potentially present a large volume of information, would it be used by learners? It would need to be integrated with the other material within the package. However, since this is likely to be spread over several screen displays learners need to move freely between the different elements, rather like holding the pages of a book open with their fingers to allow them to compare different pages. This is more difficult to achieve on the screen than in a book. In general it is best to avoid this type of design. Each illustration is more likely to assist learning where it is employed on its own with relevant support material.

So far we have largely considered a dynamic display where images can grow in size and multiple frames of the learning material are linked to the initial display. If we consider a static display, what would be the effect of adding extra images? A single illustration will probably be studied in reasonable detail, so a designer can be assured it will be an effective use of the resource. A display of two images will offer two focii for learners to choose between. Both are likely to be considered by the learners. However, three or more images increase the risk of attention being divided and less information being extracted from the illustration. This is similar reasoning to the overuse of colour or other devices. Try to resist the temptation to over-employ any approach. To show more than three images on a static display will probably result in some not being analysed. To reduce this effect integrate text with each image or use exercises to encourage the study of each image. However, it is good practice to avoid using more than three images in a single display.

Icons and buttons

One of the commonest control/navigation features of computer systems are icons or buttons which provide links with other parts of the system. The user clicks on the icon/button with the mouse pointer or by using the keyboard. Icons are usually of three types (see Figure 7.10):

- a word or phrase
- a picture
- a mixture of words and pictures.

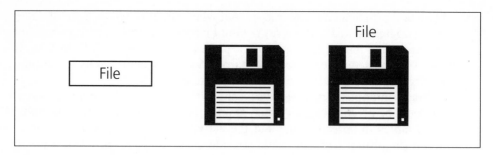

Figure 7.10   Types of icon

The users' comprehension of the three types of icon is critical when they are making their choice of action. The system will not be enhanced if the users are not clear of an icon's meaning. They will make mistakes and perhaps be unable to recover from them.

Mixed word–picture icons provide two channels of communication, a word and a picture. Where abbreviations are employed as the word component of the icon, due to lack of space, it is vital that they are understood by the users. Best practice is to use the full word whenever possible.

Whatever type of icon or button is used learners must know that they have clicked on them successfully. For example, when you click on it, it changes. The commonest change is simply to move like a physical button or switch.

The design of meaningful icons is important. Here are some guidelines for developing icons and buttons:

● The size of button or icon depends on how they will be activated. Will your learners click on them with an on-screen pointer (for example, a mouse), a hand held device (for example, a pen) or their finger? If they are using their finger then the icon or button needs to be larger than the other two. Figure 7.11 shows an example of the relative sizes for a hand held device, an on-screen pointer and a finger (left to right).

● Use standard icons or buttons if they already exist in preference to developing new images (for example, underlining words on websites is now widely accepted as indicating a hypertext link or button).

● Use familiar images (Figure 7.12 shows a simplified dictionary).

● Relate icon images to the function they provide and the learning subject.

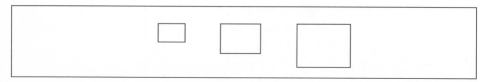

Figure 7.11   Relative sizes of icon or button

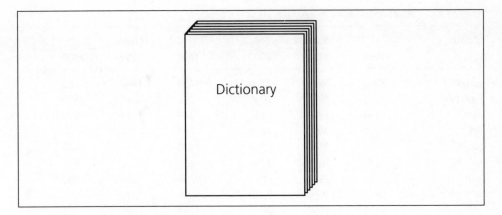

Figure 7.12   Familiar image icon

- Be consistent in designing icons and buttons.

- Distinguish the icon and the button from the rest of the display – for example, by enclosing it in a box or employing another highlighting device. Microsoft Word annotates icons when the mouse pointer crosses them and depresses them when the mouse is clicked.

Captions

In a workbook, illustrations are often given captions to help learners understand their content. In computer-based learning the display of text is more limited so the caption may be the only text linked to the illustration on screen. Captions can take many forms but tend to be descriptions of the image. They help learners to understand the illustration and also to extract the information which they contain. Captions may also provide an exercise linked to the illustration. This ensures interaction of the learners with the image so that its value is fully accessed by them. Table 7.1 shows an example of an exercise and description linked to a logical image.

Exercises have the additional advantage of assisting the interaction between learners and the learning material.

Lines, borders and frames

The layout of information on the screen can be improved by the use of lines, borders and frames to separate parts of the screen and the information.

Lines can be used for several purposes. They can separate information, divide

Table 7.1   *Illustration linked to exercise*

Month	Sales			Costs		
	1998	**1999**	**2000**	**1998**	**1999**	**2000**
January	2000	1950	2200	1470	1490	1560
February	1980	1805	2090	1230	1340	1530
March	1990	1970	2100	1360	1510	1570
April	1930	2090	2030	1290	1340	1580
May	1870	2100	2250	1420	1320	1540
June	1970	2050	2190	1410	1230	1610
July	2030	1990	2060	1390	1570	1500
August	1870	1950	2200	1280	1230	1490
September	1890	1950	2030	1350	1190	1510
October	2000	2100	2300	1610	1320	1425
November	2010	2280	2130	1250	1240	1325
December	1980	2470	2240	1340	1360	1500

Exercise
Table 7.1 shows the annual sales and costs of a product over a three-year period. Analyse the data to determine whether the product is becoming more or less profitable and offer an explanation. What was (a) the most profitable year and (b) the least profitable month over the three years?
Description
Table 7.1 shows the relationship between sales and costs on a monthly basis over a three-year period between 1998 and 2000. You can see the patterns of costs and sales against time.

the display into distinct areas, highlight areas of the material or individual words and when used in groups provide useful perceptual images. Figure 7.13 shows the effect of using multiple lines of different thicknesses thin to thick, thick to thin and random. Systematically increasing or decreasing line thickness is a way of showing depth and also of drawing the learners' attention.

   Surrounding information and command features (for example, menus) with borders or frames serves to focus users' attention on them. They also separate a feature from the rest of the display. Users should be able to identify features easily. Borders are a useful device for highlighting navigation elements (for example, buttons).

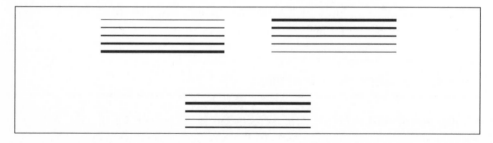

Figure 7.13   **Examples of lines**

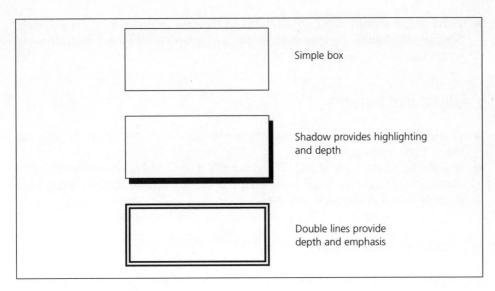

Figure 7.14   Examples of boxes

Enclosing areas in boxes helps to draw the learners' attention. It can be used to emphasize information (for example, cases studies or questions). Figure 7.14 shows examples of simple ways of enclosing information.

The graphic elements of a display can be emphasized by making them appear closer to the user, particularly useful in displays employing windows. A number of techniques can be used to provide depth, including:

- overlapping
- shadows
- highlighting
- growing
- bevelled edges.

Remember, in order to get the best out of lines, borders and frames or other devices to add depth use them sparingly and consistently. The heavy application of any of these devices will produce a cluttered display which will only serve to distract and confuse learners.

Summary of key points

General issues

- Illustrations of all types are powerful learning aids.
- Learning illustrations can be classified according to their role in learning into three types: representative/realistic, analogical and logical.

- Illustrations should be closely related to the text in order to assist learning. Simply displaying images which do not relate to the text will not aid learning.

Realistic illustrations

- A highly realistic illustration is a powerful motivator but tends to hide the detail from learners.
- Simplified images are useful in focusing learners' attention on the key elements. The degree of detail in an image is closely related to the instructional purpose that it is intended to serve.

Analogical illustrations

- An analogy is a powerful way of relating learners' previous knowledge to the learning material.
- The successful use of analogies is dependent on learners recognizing the image as an analogy. If they fail to realize it they can become confused or distracted.

Logical illustrations

- Logical images are very useful in computer-based learning which is not an ideal environment for text. Logical illustrations (for example, charts and tables) can present a large volume of information in a small area.
- The value of logical illustrations is dependent on the learners' willingness to study the image and extract its content.
- Graphical organizers provide learners with a structure on which to base new information.

Multiple illustrations

- Learners are unlikely to study in detail more than three images on a single display.

Icons and buttons

- The meaningfulness of icons and buttons is critical to their success.
- A mixed word and picture icon is likely to be easier to understand than picture or word icons on their own.

Captions

- Two main types of caption used in computer-based learning are descriptive and exercise.
- Exercises help learners to understand the nature of logical images by ensuring they study the key details.

Lines, borders and frames

- Lines, borders and frames are powerful aids to structuring, displaying and emphasizing key issues. They should not be over-used.

Reference

Alesandrini, K.L. (1987), 'Computer Graphics in Learning and Instruction', *The Psychology of Illustration*, vol. 2, H.A. Houghton and D.M. Willows (eds), Springer-Verlag, pp. 159–88.

Chapter 8

Multimedia

By the end of this chapter you will have been introduced to:

- what is multimedia?
- multimedia and learning
- hypermedia
- video
- sound
- dynamic display
- animation
- combining different media
- disabled learners.

Multimedia and learning

People interact with the environment through their senses of sight, hearing, touch, taste and smell. It is widely accepted in conventional education and training that learning methods should seek to incorporate as many senses as possible. For example:

- cooks learn through taste and smell
- engineers are encouraged to touch and feel objects
- mechanics detect faults through careful listening as well as through observation.

Multimedia in computer-based learning aims to include as many senses in the experience as possible and thus to make it more effective. For most people communication with their world is mainly through sight, while hearing, touch, smell and taste are secondary, if important, sources of information. In particular situations, however, each sense may become the key communication channel.

Multimedia is normally defined as a mixture of three or more of the following:

- digital video
- sound
- graphics
- text
- animation
- still photographs.

In practice, there is no standard which defines the relative amounts of the different media. It does not incorporate touch, taste or smell which largely remain outside of multimedia design (although touch can be added through the use of virtual reality techniques employing data gloves or other devices).

Different media have been used to enhance open and distance learning materials for many years and packages have often combined workbooks, video tapes, audio tapes and practical kits (for example, to carry out experiments). Practical kits can incorporate touch, taste and smell into the learning experience. Computer-based multimedia does not normally include practical kits, but on-screen simulations fulfil their role. Multimedia frequently includes a workbook, even if this is little more than an introduction to the package.

Human tutors are not restricted to a single medium. They use a variety of methods to communicate to a student, including their voice combined with body movements to emphasize points and a range of visual aids such as overhead projector slides. They will give students summaries, examples of objects and even take them on visits to directly experience an environment. This is a multimedia approach.

In a similar way computer-based multimedia is trying to capture the same learning experience through the computer screen, but we should not deceive ourselves that we can provide an identical experience. Nevertheless, this realization should not stop us aiming to achieve the highest standards. Video can provide some of the features of a site visit, at a lower cost and it is always available, whereas a real visit needs special arrangements. Speech and sound can emulate a tutor's voice so that enthusiasm can be communicated to the student. Text can present the details of the subject. Tutors get tired and have good and bad days. High quality multimedia and computer-based learning in general provide a consistent experience and are always available.

Hypermedia

Hypermedia is multimedia based on a hypertext system in which users navigate their way through the material by clicking on links which are provided by individual words or phrases. Each link moves them between chunks of text. A hypermedia system is not restricted to text. Links and chunks of information can be provided by many different media. An image can be a link to text, text linked

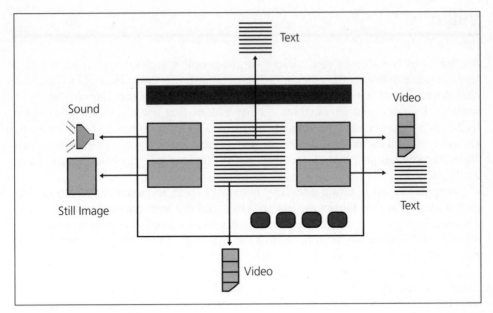

Figure 8.1   **Hypermedia**

to a picture, a picture to speech, text to video, video to an animation or any other combinations. All combinations are possible so you are creating an exciting environment which has the potential to combine the best of multimedia to present information with the freedom to choose provided by hypertext.

Figure 8.1 illustrates the different links. A hypermedia system can in fact be far richer than this simple image would indicate, since it appears to limit the system to one link while in practice there is no limit. A link in a column of text can generate a picture which can, in turn, link to sounds or video. The series of connections can be extensive, depending on the subject and your objective.

The complexity of hypermedia is both a main factor in its potential for enhancing learning and also its main risk when developing this type of system. Learners can find the different media combined with the normal issues of getting lost or confused by navigating through a hypertext system bewildering. There is the considerable danger of making it too difficult for learners to navigate the system. The key is to use the different media and links to support clear learning objectives and enrich the learning opportunities. For example, an engineering text can allow users to see photographs of the actual equipment described, hear the people involved speak and read additional background information. From a relatively dry text, you can create a highly motivating experience.

Hypermedia provides a rich information environment for learners, but it is important for them to know when they have exhausted all the material. This can be difficult since the subject they are studying is likely to be new to them. You must provide clear guidance about what they should achieve, either in the form of instructions, questions, or a combination of both.

Video

We are a highly video-literate society – most people watch television, view video tapes at home and visit the cinema. Some of us also use video cameras to produce our own record of holidays or family events. This degree of familiarity is likely to result in learners who expect high quality videos that use television production techniques. Learners will be critical of videos which fail to reach these standards and will not find them helpful. The positive effects, however, are that learners will understand techniques such as flashbacks, split screens, overlays and documentary methods.

Computer-based learning normally integrates short sequences of video lasting only a minute or two within the material to avoid the learners passively watching a scene. The design must ensure that learners can successfully interact with these sequences, by allowing them to control the showing of the video. Controls on the screen are similar to those on a videoplayer (see Figure 8.2).

Learners can pause, rewind or fast forward the video so that they can study the material in the detail they require. This control can be linked to the content of the learning material by asking the learners to make decisions based on what they have seen. The feedback in response to their answer can be another sequence of video or other media. Figure 8.3 shows an example display. This is a useful way of providing feedback to the learners especially in the context of management of staff, customer relations and interpersonal skills. Good practice can be reinforced or a poor decision challenged by the feedback video.

Video, however, uses large amounts of memory which tends to restrict its use. Compromises have to be made, such as the size of the image shown or a reduced frame rate. Frequently, video is displayed in a small window so that the images only occupy a proportion of the screen (one-quarter or one-eighth of the screen is the minimum which should be used). This reduces the memory/storage problems but at the expense of reducing the impact of the video. Another technique is to base the video on a slow frame rate. Video consists of individual frames which are run one after another to produce the effect of a moving image. Television uses a frame rate of either 25 or 30 frames per second. A minute of video needs 1500/1800 frames and thus a very large amount of memory. If the frame rate is

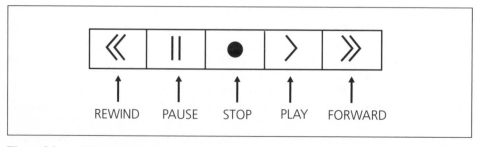

Figure 8.2   Video controls

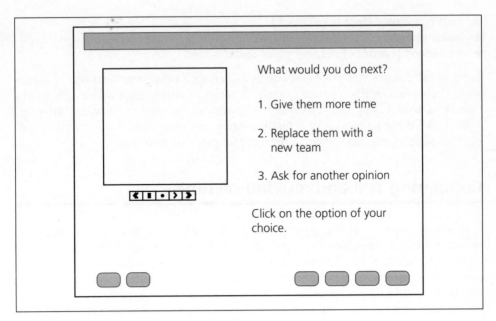

Figure 8.3   Video interface

reduced then considerable amounts of memory can be saved, but if there are fewer frames it is more difficult to capture movements without the image breaking up and not being fluid. This often results in multimedia products with video which are simply the head and shoulders of a person speaking to the camera. Action sequences are not used. Such compromises can effectively reduce the value of video to a point where it should not be used. Video is very expensive to develop and thus you must have strong reasons to include it your computer-based learning materials. Remember these compromises will destroy its value.

Computer technology is improving rapidly so the use of video is becoming more straightforward and the need for these compromises will soon be eliminated. However, it is still an important consideration, especially in relation to online learning material. The bandwidth available is very limited so that incorporating video is difficult or even impossible. It is normally achieved by using streaming technology or by downloading compressed files, enabling the video to run on the learner's computer rather than over the network.

Video should always be compared with other media regarding its ability to convey a particular message. If you going to show a head and shoulders video to explain a point, would a still photograph and recorded speech or even a simple text message achieve the same result? Does the impact of the video justify the extra costs? Some effective uses of video, with examples, include:

- action (showing how to use a hand tool)
- human–human interaction (serving a customer)

- context/environment (workplace)
- industrial processes (making steel)
- hazardous practices (welding pipes under water).

Even in these cases it is always worth considering if other combinations of media would achieve a similar or better result. A series of still images with a voice-over can be a useful way of delivering information. A minute of video (that is, 1500/1800 image frames) may actually contain relatively little content while a single still photograph can convey a meaningful piece of information.

Comparing still and moving pictures

It is always worth comparing still images with video. Both have strengths and weaknesses and the application and context need to be considered to identify appropriate uses. Table 8.1 provides a summary of the comparison. Video is a powerful motivator and particularly useful at showing human interactions and action. However, it is expensive to produce and requires expertise to use effectively. Still images can communicate considerable content and are cheap and easy to produce, but they have limited value in showing action sequences.

Table 8.1   *Comparison of still images and video*

Features	Still images	Video
Information	Can convey detailed information	Short sequences of video convey little information
Motivation	Can create interest in topic	Powerful motivator
Interaction	Needs to be integrated into material	Needs to be integrated into material
Action/Process	Limited value in portraying action or processes	Potentially effective in showing action and process
Quality	Even poor quality or simplified images can be useful	Learners expect high quality
Production	Straightforward to produce	Time consuming and requires considerable expertise to produce
Cost	Low cost	High cost
Interpersonal	Weak at showing relationships unless multiple stills are used	Strong at showing human-to-human relationships

A technique often used in television to convey a video-type story is the linking of a series of still images with a commentary and music to create a suitable atmosphere. It may tell the story of a historical event where video is not available. It is often effective and is similar to a training technique known as a tape/slide presentation where a series of 35mm slides is synchronized with a taped voice-over. In multimedia this can be an effective approach. If you wanted to develop the awareness of hazards in an industrial environment, you can show a series of still images and ask learners to identify which are potentially dangerous.

Sound

One aspect of video which is often ignored is the use of sound or speech. Sound is very useful in multimedia to convey information and to create a learning atmosphere. It adds considerable value to video or still photographs. Even on its own it is valuable. The uses of sound and speech include:

- helping to create a suitable atmosphere for the learning material
- gaining the learners' attention
- providing a wide range of feedback
- providing a source of additional information rather like annotating a document with margin notes
- providing examples (recording of famous voices, machinery sounds and so on)
- reinforcing warning messages
- personalizing the material (by using the learner's name)
- adding sound captions to illustrations
- supporting learners with visual impairments by reading the display to them.

Sounds are also used to provide feedback or to attract users' attention. When you enter information using a keyboard you can hear that you have pressed a key. When a warning message appears on the screen it is often accompanied with a sound effect (for example, a bleep or a bell) to attract attention to the message. In multimedia systems, these can be employed to draw attention to key learning points. These sound effects, however, can be very irritating if over-used. If a recording of applause is played every time learners get an answer right, it will soon cease to have a positive effect. Learners should be given control over sound effects so that they can turn them off and on. Remember to tell learners to switch on the sound when they first use a product otherwise they may be unaware that they are missing the sound content of a package.

Sound is only effective in assisting learning if learners are able to concentrate on the speech, sound effect or music. Most people are skilled at not listening because of the noisy world in which we all live. To survive in a modern society which bombards us with lift music, telephone systems and voice-overs, we need to learn to ignore sounds, which unfortunately makes the task of using sound in multimedia learning material more difficult.

By selecting sounds carefully you can influence the mood of learners. Sounds can convey mental images so you can make learners feel they are in an office, industrial situation or countryside by playing them typical sounds of that environment. This is useful in helping learners make the connections between the content of learning material and their previous experience. In a way it is similar to using an analogical image to help learners relate their prior learning to the new content.

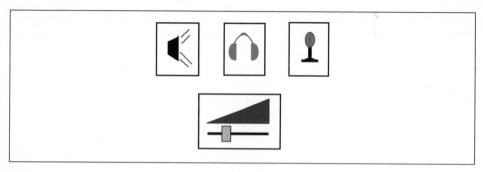

Figure 8.4   Speech and volume icons

If learners do not perceive the link, they may be puzzled by the sounds. Background music can also contribute to creating a particular atmosphere. However, people's choice of music varies considerably and you do not want to create telephone queuing or lift music. If you employ background music, you must provide the means of switching it off as with other sound effects.

Speech can provide an additional source of information – for example, by explaining a photograph or providing an alternative explanation to the displayed text. It is often most effective as an extra feature rather than as the principal method of presenting information. In a similar way to video, the danger is that it will encourage a passive approach to the material and thus it should be integrated with interactive features. The learners must be given control of the commentary so that they can listen to it as many times as they require or indeed choose not to listen to it at all. This is most easily achieved by providing an icon which shows learners that a commentary is available (see Figure 8.4). The learners also need to be given control of the volume. This could be by means of a small icon with a slider (see Figure 8.4). The quality and nature of the speech also conveys a message to the learners, in that a monotone voice will not motivate them to listen. It is vital that the voice communicates interest, excitement and commitment to the subject to help motivate the learners.

The disadvantages of using speech and sound include the following:

- Information is more difficult to remember than other media since it is more transitory.
- Repetitive sounds and speech can be irritating.

These disadvantages underline the premise that learners must be able to control the speech and sound as well as use it as an additional source of information to reinforce other media (for example, text and illustrations).

Speech is produced in a variety of ways in computer systems, including:

- speech synthesis
- prerecorded messages
- concatenation (that is, short bits of prerecorded speech pasted together to create a sentence).

Computer-based learning tends to use prerecorded messages which is the best way of ensuring the highest quality of speech. The human ear is very sensitive and can detect even modest compromises on sound quality. Concatenation can produce speech that is often lacking the correct tone or emphasis. Although speech synthesis has improved, it is still of limited quality. In order to design speech input you should:

● write for listening not reading
● keep speech input short so that it is easy to remember
● use questions to engage the learner and provide interaction.

Speech input is rarely used in multimedia except when the subject is learning a new language. In this case it allows learners to practise their speech. The main approach is to ask the learners to listen to some speech in the new language and either to repeat the speech or respond to it as if they are conducting a conversation. The learners can replay their efforts and judge their own success.

Dynamic display

A useful attribute of the computer screen is that it is a dynamic environment. We have often described the design of a display in a way that implies that it is static and fixed like a book page but nothing is further from the truth. The whole or part of a display can change. Many different visual effects can be used to alter the display. The screen can be wiped from top or bottom and right or left or sucked down a hole in the middle. These effects can add interest to the presentation but their overuse can irritate and distract.

Windows which present information are another example of the dynamic nature of the screen. A window can grow, shrink and be minimized. Text can be static or scroll up and down and left and right. Text can be presented inside windows or outside of them. Graphic images can be minimized as an icon which, when clicked on, will grow to a size that can be studied. Thus a library of images can be displayed on a single screen to present a wide range of examples of a subject. Objects on the screen can also be manipulated, dragged and dropped into new positions or even removed from the display. This is an exciting environment in which to design learning materials. However, the danger is that by providing a highly visual dynamic display, the learners may become overloaded and distracted from the key learning objectives.

Animation

Animation provides an attractive visual stimulus to enliven a dull subject, but you must take care that it aids learning. Some operating systems use animation to show processes which are normally invisible (for example, copying a computer file).

This is a useful way of reinforcing a learning experience. The way to copy files could be described in text with perhaps an optional commentary, while the animation provides the visual component.

There are a variety of forms of animation ranging from the professional cartoon, which is extremely time consuming and expensive to produce, to an image which changes when the learners move their mouse pointer across it. The latter is often used on websites to enhance a text display but can also emphasize an area of the display. As the pointer enters the image or area it is highlighted or replaced with another image. When the pointer leaves, the display reverts back to its original form. This method encourages learners to explore a display and find interesting pieces of information hidden in it. A map can be enhanced by this technique so that you can find additional information hidden in the different parts of the overall image.

A simple and long established way of providing animation is by drawing pictures on cards which are each slightly different from the previous one by rapidly flicking the cards, the picture seems to change. This can easily be accomplished by a computer without the large costs of professional animation. Nevertheless, even a short sequence will take a considerable amount of effort to develop.

Animation is effective when it is used:

- in a straightforward way linked directly to the learning objectives of the material
- in short sequences (rather like video) so that learners are not reduced to passive spectators
- to support, or be supported by, other media (for example, commentary related to animation or text related to animation)
- under the learners' control so that they pause, rewind, fast forward and stop the display in similar way to controlling video
- to draw the learners' attention to a particular area of the display or to emphasize key issues.

Whilst these are similar points to the use of video, the main difference is in those subject areas where animation can provide something new. Animation is good at allowing learners to analyse any action which happens too fast to follow with the eye, such as the leg movements of a running animal. It is equally effective in showing an event which happens over a long period, such as the flowering of a plant. In both cases learners can alter the pace of the event by slowing down or speeding up the action. Animation is also useful in revealing scenes which are too small to be seen, such as subatomic particles, or providing a visual image of a process which is normally invisible.

Figure 8.5 shows a frame-by-frame animation under the learners' control where they can interact with a process and study each tiny element of which it is composed. In this case it is movements of the body, but it could be the flow of a liquid, the movement of molecules or the aerodynamics of an object.

The control over the animation is provided by a simple bar. By dragging the slider, learners can speed up or slow down the pace of the display and by clicking

Figure 8.5   Control of animation

on arrows they can move the animation forward or back a small step at a time. Other ways of controlling an animation include a list of different speed options from which learners select. The control of video has been transferred from the video recorder but it could be used for animation control. Sounds could be adapted to provide on and off with a volume controller. The choice should reflect the learning objectives and nature of the subject.

Combining different media

A key issue in developing a multimedia system for learning material is deciding which media to use. Each has different strengths and weaknesses. Table 8.2 summarizes some of their key learning points.

Each medium is treated in the table as a separate entity, while in multimedia they ideally provide mutual support. Different media can particularly reinforce each other, such as:

- sound and video
- text and pictures
- speech and still photographs
- text, illustrations and speech
- animation and text.

This mutual support assumes that each medium is carrying the same or related information. If they provide different content, then the result is confusion – rather like two tutors making a presentation in the same room at the same time on different subjects.

Individual learning styles often relate to a particular medium; for example, some people prefer to learn by reading text while others like a high visual content.

Table 8.2   *Comparison of different media*

Medium	Strength	Weakness
Text	Presentation of detailed content Can be highly structured to divide a subject into meaningful parts Easy to integrate with other media	Poor readability on the screen compared to paper
Video	Realism can be provided Presents true environments without having to visit them Motivational Effective at presenting interpersonal interaction	High quality is expected Expensive to produce Limited content
Sound	Creates an atmosphere Integrates well with other media (e.g. text and images) Sound effects can be an effective form of feedback	Overuse can irritate
Animation	Motivational Can present events too small or difficult to see (e.g. subatomic) Attentional device	Very expensive to produce high quality sequences
Graphics	Key points can be isolated and clarified Add interest Aid recall	Need to relate to text and other content Learners need to identify image (e.g. analogies)
Colour	Motivation and interest is increased Captures attention Emphasis	Overuse can distract and hinder learning Colour blindness
Still photographs	Realism is presented in a low cost way Aid motivation Rich in content Aid recall	Need to relate to text and other content High quality expected

Users learning about a subject should have a choice between different combinations of media. Many websites offer users the alternative of a text only display or one combining text and illustrations. In a learning package users can listen to a commentary while watching a video or studying an image. The two media reinforce each other and do not hinder. Learner control over the various media is important to allow for different learning styles.

The danger of combining different media is that although you have created a rich, exciting learning environment, you may overload learners with stimuli. They will be unable to identify the key issues in the mass of information which is available to them. Effective integration of the media is more important than development of a rich environment.

Disabled learners

When designing multimedia systems, it is important to consider their potential for disabled learners. Many learners access computers through technology such as screen readers, speech input devices and specialized interfaces. This allows them to overcome the barriers of being unable to see the display or use input devices such as a mouse. It is worth seeking specialist advice about how your product can be inclusive rather than exclusive.

Always provide a text equivalent of the different media, since a number of devices make the material accessible to disabled learners through the use of text. A screen reader can read the text to learners by synthesizing it into speech. A spoken commentary may be a useful way of accessing the material. Remember that a sound track of a video normally does not describe the scene, so you may need to enhance the sound to provide a description. For learners with hearing impairments the sound should be duplicated as text, so they can read the content of the video sound track.

Before you begin to design your multimedia package, investigate ways in which you can widen access to your material. There are a variety of standards available, in some cases concentrating on the World Wide Web.

Summary of key points

General issues

- Multimedia is a mixture of three or more media such as video, sound, graphics, text, animation and still photographs.
- Multimedia is based on engaging a range of the learners' senses.
- Hypermedia is multimedia with a hypertext structure.
- The complexity of multimedia both enhances its potential to assist learning and also runs the risk of confusing learners. A clear integration of the different media is more likely to be successful than a media-rich learning environment.

Video

- Learners expect high quality video.
- Video is a powerful motivator.
- Learners must have considerable control over the video display.
- Video is expensive to produce so you should have distinct reasons for including it. It is best to compare video with other media such as still images.

Sound

- Sound effects and speech are very effective in adding value to other media such as text or still images.
- Sound effects reinforce other attentional devices.
- Sound effects can create a learning atmosphere.
- Repetitive sounds or speech can irritate.
- Quality of speech depends heavily on the technological approach taken (for example, prerecorded or concatenation).
- Learners must have control of sound effects and speech.

Dynamic display

- The computer provides an exciting creative environment for the design of learning material. Take care that learners are not overloaded with stimuli.

Animation

- Animation can bring alive non-visual subjects (for example, quantum physics).
- Animations aids learning if it is used in short sequences, in addition to other media and in a straightforward way.
- Learners must have control over the animation.

Combining different media

- Media must be effectively integrated.

Chapter 9

Online learning design

By the end of this chapter you will have been introduced to:

- online learning materials
- structure of a website
- use of metaphors
- hypertext links
- designing a webpage
- how to judge the length of a webpage
- page layout
- problems of being lost in hyperspace
- different types of communication technologies
- vicarious learning.

Online material and other forms of computer-based learning

Online learning material can take many forms. It may simply be a means of distributing learning products by allowing geographically scattered learners to print out webpages or download files of computer-based learning. Other online materials can be accessed on websites but you should never forget that many learners may wish to study the material on the screen and as printed documents. Materials should be designed as either conventional paper-based open learning or computer-based learning.

Designers of online material must remember that learners will be accessing the website through a range of browsers which they will configure to meet their individual needs. Studies have shown that users are very influenced in their attitude to online material by the speed at which they can access it, which will depend to a large extent on the learners' telecommunication link. You will probably not know what browser or telecommunication link learners will be using.

They could include the following:

- a low-speed modem link, a basic computer and a text-only browser
- a broadband high-speed link, a high specification computer and the latest browser
- a standard configuration because they all work for the same company
- many different configurations because they are individuals who are learning at home
- applications which will read the display to them if they are visually impaired. In this case images will have a very limited impact and can be puzzling because their reading systems can only tell them that there is an image, not what it is.

Most online designs are a compromise, often providing learners with access to more than one version of the design in order to broaden the use of the material (for example, text only or text and illustrations). A good practice is to state clearly for what technology the site has been optimized or for whom the site has been designed. It is always wise to view your webpages through a variety of browsers and computers. Your choice of fonts may look good when viewed on your own computers but will they be available on your learners' computers? If they are not, then other fonts will appear. Your layout may look effective when you designed it, but your learners may need to scroll horizontally to read the text. This will cause them considerable problems in following your arguments, since to read each line of text will necessitate scrolling right and left.

Online learning material normally comprises many pages and the time taken to move between them varies according to the nature of the users' technology. Even a short delay can break learners' concentration. The aim is to move between different sections almost instantaneously, but this is almost impossible to achieve even employing high-speed links. At best it takes several seconds to change pages, at worst a minute or longer. There is also no guarantee that the link will not be broken and the learner forced to reconnect. Your design should allow for these delays.

Another choice for designers is to allow learners to print out the learning material as standalone documents. The webpages can be printed or files can be attached to the pages, which learners can download and print or view locally. Webpages that are likely to be printed should be as effective a learning experience as paper-based material. On-screen colour can highlight text, but when printed out it can considerably reduce the legibility of the text. There are other examples where designing for the screen compromises a paper-based design. Always test your design in both media to ensure it is effective.

Comparing Internet, intranet and standalone materials

Table 9.1 provides comparison of the issues of developing learning material which will be accessed from a website, the organization's own intranet or on an

Table 9.1   *Comparison of Internet, intranet and standalone materials*

Factor	Internet website	Intranet	Standalone computer
Administration	Easy to know who and how many are using the package	Easy to know who and how many are using the package	You can control number of copies issued but do not know who is using them or how many
Version control	Easy to update since essentially only one copy	Easy to update since essentially only one copy	Previous version must be recalled to allow new version to be released or learners need to check they have the latest version Cost of issuing new version relatively high
Access	Widely available and learners have freedom of location (e.g. workplace, learning centre, cybercafé, home)	Widely available within organization (e.g. workplace and learning centre)	Limited by the need to have a physical copy of product
Content	Limited bandwidth constrains the use of multimedia	Bandwidth is a factor to consider but multimedia can be employed in many cases	Multimedia is the norm
Changes	Low cost, quick and easy to make all forms of changes	Low cost, quick and easy to make all forms of changes	Need to be significant to justify the cost of a new edition of the edition (e.g. cost of 1000 CD ROMs)
Speed	Can be slow when moving between different elements which can break learners' concentration	Small time differences when switching between elements are possible but are usually not significant	Fast, efficient and effective
Communication	Many possibilities of enriching the package by integrating links to other learners, mentors and to expert assistance	Potentially similar to an Internet-based package, but occasionally with few other students and no inhouse expertise	Normally not a feature
Interactivity	Due to limitations of communicating with a website interactivity is reduced, although good design can reduce effects	No significant limitations except the imagination of the designer	No significant limitations expect the imagination of the designer

individual computer (for example, by CD-ROM). This is a complex choice which depends on the nature of the material and the designer's objectives. A volatile subject is perhaps best served by an online solution since this is straightforward and low cost to maintain, enhance and amend. CD-ROM or other forms of standalone product are able to incorporate all forms of multimedia which will be constrained by the bandwidth limitations of online solutions, although an intranet-based package can also employ multimedia. Online packages can exploit their communication potential to add value to the material which is not normally available to a standalone package.

Structure of a website

The nature of a website depends on what you are aiming to achieve. In simple terms, you have two main choices – a deep or shallow site. Figure 9.1 shows a deep site with several levels and complex navigation, providing the learners with many choices and the potential for rich interactions. There is a danger, however, that learners will become disoriented and lost within the structure.

At the other extreme is a shallow site shown in Figure 9.2. This is a simple design with little risk of disorientation but with minimum choice and basic inter-action.

The main dangers when designing websites are that the learners will either become lost or find the design lacking in interest, challenge and motivation. The best practice is to choose a design that mirrors the nature of the learning subject. In that way learning is reinforced and navigation is more predictable. Worst

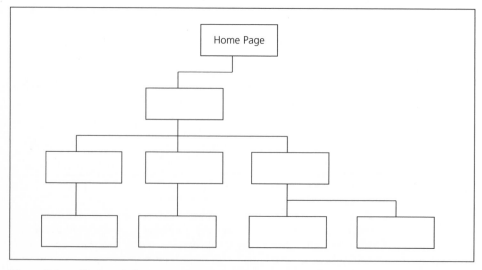

Figure 9.1   Deep website

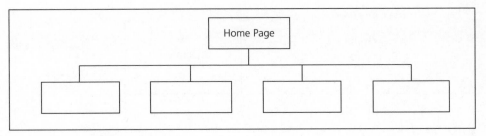

Figure 9.2   Shallow website

practice is simply to develop the site as you go along without an overall plan or style to guide you.

Metaphors

A useful way to aid learners' navigation of online materials is to employ an over-all design metaphor. The metaphor should be familiar to the learners so that they are able to predict the nature of the material. A book metaphor suggests that the learning material is divided into chapters, will contain a contents list and an index and perhaps a glossary of terms and bibliography. Since learners are familiar with books, they are aware that the material is organized in a linear manner but with a freedom to browse.

If you were developing a package for learners who are familiar with a training centre you may use that as a metaphor. A training centre might consist of lecture theatres, resource centre or library, notice boards, trainer's office, administration office and rest room. This model might turn:

- the lecture theatre into the area where learners can access tutorial material
- the resource centre or library into the reference material area
- the notice board into the frequently asked questions area so that users can share the answers to everyone's questions
- the trainer's office into an e-mail link to tutors who can answer questions about the topic
- the administration office into the trainees' records of progress, and a means of booking a place on the course and paying for the service
- the rest room into an area where trainees can communicate with, and support, each other.

Trainees with experience of a conventional training centre are likely to find this online learning approach straightforward to adapt to, easy to navigate and pre-dictable. They should not get lost within the system. A map of the website would resemble the floor plan of a training centre and learners could access the different components by linking each room with the related learning areas (see Figure 9.3).

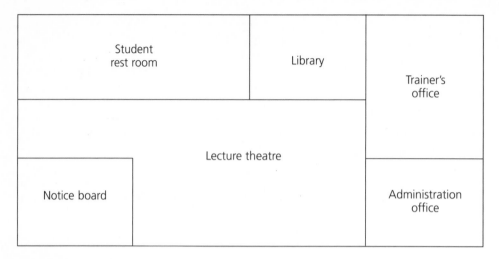

Figure 9.3   Training centre map

Links

One important factor of good online learning materials is the design of the hypertext links. The overall look and feel of the package is to a large extent dependent on the number, design and structure of the links. Hypertext links are very easy to create so there is a danger of producing material which has too many connections and no overall structure, with the result that it confuses and disorients the learners.

You must have a distinct purpose for creating a link and an overall strategy for their use in the learning design. Some reasons for the creation of a link are to:

- provide additional information and examples so that learners can probe the topic in greater depth
- cross-reference items
- instruct learners to carry out a task (for example, a form of help)
- provide a help system
- provide a glossary
- provide footnotes
- provide contents lists
- provide illustrations to support text
- provide text to support an illustration
- connect the different aspects of a topic (similar to an index).

Hypertext links allow designers to escape from linear designs and provide more imaginative and exciting material. Beware a 'scatter gun' approach which will simply confuse learners. Links offer a more flexible approach to design by enabling learners to choose a route through the material. To benefit from this advantage learners must understand the nature of hypertext, what they are

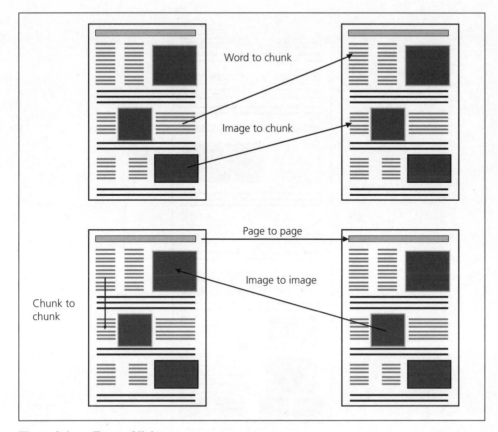

Figure 9.4   Types of link

searching for and what objectives they hope to achieve. Random browsing may be interesting and may produce serendipitous results but it is often ineffective.

There are a range of different types of link (see Figure 9.4) including:

- a single word to a chunk of information
- one information chunk to another chunk
- a word to a whole website
- one webpage to another page
- an image to a chunk of information
- one image to another.

Designers should provide each link with a clear relationship between its starting and finishing points so learners can predict how they work. One approach is to ensure that the links follow the standards of the World Wide Web in so far as it has standards. The Web has many common practices which essentially have become standards. One simple practice is to underline word links and to change the colour of the word or the line or both once they have been activated.

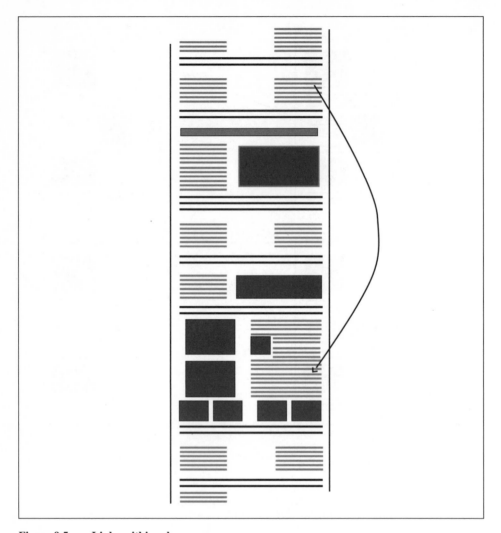

Figure 9.5   Links within a long page

Links not only connect different pages but also parts of the same page (see Figure 9.5). In a long page links are essential in order to navigate the information, but if a page is too long they can be confusing. Learners may not be aware if a link will move them to a new page or to another part of the same page. It is normal practice to provide 'Top of Page' links at intervals on the page so they know how to return to the top of the page.

In designing a same page link remember that the learner will only see part of the page and can therefore easily become lost. To reduce this risk make links returnable, employ 'Top of Page' links and draw learners' attention to the browser's standard forward and back functions.

Page length

Computer-based learning is often described in terms of a single-screen display called a frame with designs often based around individual frames and their connections. In contrast, webpages are usually longer than a single-screen display and in some ways resemble a printed page. There is no standard length for a web-page and it is not unusual to find examples of pages of twenty or more frames. Long web pages must be scrolled up and down to access the information. Scrolling may unfortunately confuse learners and in most circumstances should be avoided or minimized. A small degree of scrolling is unlikely to be harmful to experienced computer users, but webpages frequently employ scrolling extensively.

Figure 9.6 shows the learners' view of part of a webpage. Only a part of the page is visible at any one time and as learners move up or down the view changes so they must remember the content which is out of sight. To minimize scrolling, web designers often place links within the page so that users can jump directly to another part of it. This is certainly helpful but in a very long page it is doubtful whether it will be entirely effective. Learners need to realize that they are jumping within a page not to another webpage, which is not always obvious if the page is long. To some extent this problem can be countered by providing a return link (for example, 'Top of Page').

Links within the page should be combined with other approaches to minimize confusion and to aid learners' navigation of the page, such as:

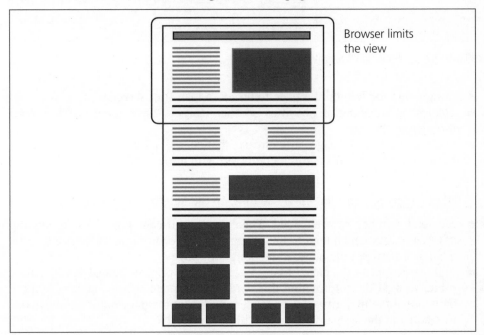

Browser limits the view

Figure 9.6   **Browser view of a webpage**

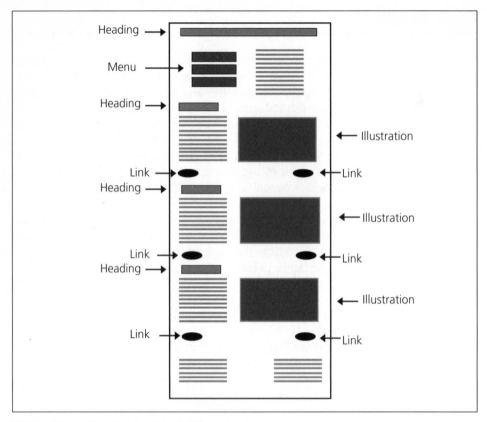

Figure 9.7   Structured webpage

- minimizing the length of a page to no more than four screens
- employing meaningful headings so that learners have points of reference throughout the page
- using a predictable page structure so that learners find it easy to navigate between sections. This is often combined with a menu of links to each section (see Figure 9.7).

Other factors to consider when deciding on the length of pages are:

- the total number of webpages. There are significant time lags in moving between pages which tend to break learners' concentration. There needs to be a balance between the number and length of pages
- will learners print the page? Many Internet users print webpages because they prefer to read the information this way. A long page is reasonable if you are certain that the majority of your readers will print the page but if many choose to read from the screen your page will be ineffective.

Page layout

On the World Wide Web users can jump directly into a website and are not limited to moving between home pages. In fact, many learners will not visit the home page and it is difficult to predict which pages they will visit. It is therefore important to make each page stand alone in providing an overview to the learning material and links to the major parts of the package. Avoid pages which are cul-de-sacs where you do not provide any links to leave the page except the forward and back browser buttons. Page design is thus an important element in designing online learning material.

When designing computer-based learning displays it is normal practice to provide a view of a screen where everything is visible to the learner. A webpage does not allow learners to see everything since only part of the page is visible as they scroll down the display – the top of the page will obviously disappear. As stated before, the learner needs to remember what has scrolled out of view.

Always provide learners with consistent features and access to the functions of the package. There are a variety of ways of offering this consistency, including:

- frames to provide access to the main parts of the package
- a menu bar across the top of the display
- standard icons and buttons throughout the site
- standard layout of pages.

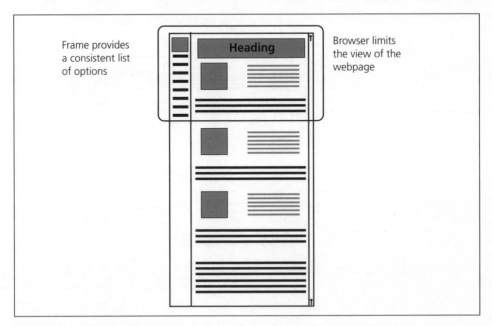

Figure 9.8   Use of frames

| Home | Text | Colour | Graphics | Glossary | Map |

Figure 9.9   Menu

Frames are a means of dividing the page into two or more areas so that one provides a constant display of options (see Figure 9.8). In a way, you are dividing the screen between the package functions and the learning content, but the negative aspect is that you sacrifice part of your display and reduce the area of content.

Menus are a standard feature of application software. Many learners are familiar with their use so providing the functions of the learning material across the top of the page is likely to be effective (see Figure 9.9).

Webpages are part of a hypertext environment which relies on the use of links to navigate the material. It is therefore important to use standard links, icons and buttons. These can take any form which you feel is appropriate but it is usual to provide:

- a standard top-of-page button or icon
- a link to the home or main page of the learning package
- links to features such as glossaries, indexes, site maps and quizzes or tests
- links, icons or buttons to the units which make up the package.

The layout should be consistent in order to help learners navigate the page (see Figure 9.10). This is most simply achieved by dividing the content into meaningful chunks of information.

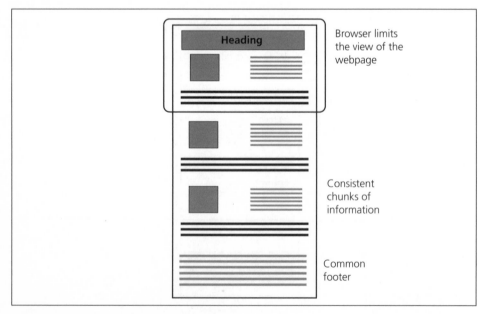

Figure 9.10   Consistent layout of webpages

Lost in hyperspace

Getting lost is a well documented phenomenon in complex hypertext systems. Questions that learners often ask themselves include:

- How did I get here?
- How do I return?
- How do I find ...?
- What else do I need to find?
- How much more information of this type is available?
- How do I quit the package?

Learners must be able to find what they are seeking in a hypertext system. They must be sure that they will not miss relevant material or waste time trying to find something that is not available. To prevent or reduce the possibilities of learners becoming disoriented or lost in hyperspace you should:

- use a straightforward structure
- use a consistent and predictable structure
- have a limited number of links
- make options available throughout the material (website) and avoid obscuring major items with minor elements
- provide standard links to:
  – home page
  – overview map
  – help system
  – index page
  – glossary
  – references
- help learners develop an accurate mental model of the site by providing an effective metaphor for the design of the material and website
- use frames to provide a permanent menu of main options on each screen display
- number pages (for example, page 2 of 10)
- use consistent topics and other names
- provide an overview map of the structure (see Figure 9.11)
- use a map icon on each page to show its position in relation to whole site (see Figure 9.12). This will aid learners who jump into the middle of the site.

Communication technologies

Online materials can be seamlessly linked to communication technologies, allowing individual learners to contact both their tutor and fellow students and support provided to them. Distance learning of all types suffers from the problem that

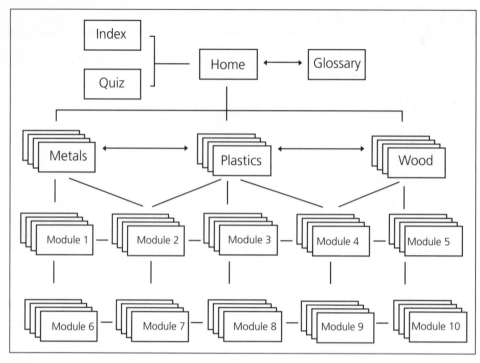

Figure 9.11   Structural map

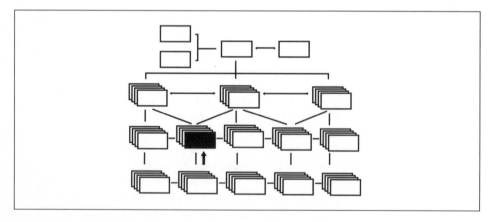

Figure 9.12   Map icon

many students fail to complete their courses. A significant factor in preventing learners dropping out is support.

Communication technologies provide high quality support to a widely dispersed audience of learners. They take two forms:

- asynchronous
- synchronous.

Asynchronous technologies do not rely on people being at either end of the communication channel. They include:

- e-mail (one-to-one or one-to-many)
- bulletin boards (many-to-many)
- mail groups (one-to-many)
- online conferences and seminars (one-to-many).

These forms of communication seem natural to use with computer-based learning, given that learners have the freedom to choose when and how they learn. E-mail is now widely used to support learners and allow them to seek help.

Synchronous technologies rely on the people being at either end of the communication channel. A telephone, for example, is synchronous but leaving a message on an answer machine is asynchronous. Synchronous technologies include:

- chat (almost entirely unevaluated as an effective means of aiding learning – one-to-one and one-to-many)
- video conferencing (one-to-one and one-to-many)
- collaborative working using groupware (groups of two or more people).

Synchronous methods are beginning to be used extensively to support learning.

Vicarious learning

Distance learning can often mean learning on your own. Individuals are isolated and do not have the benefit of interaction with other students and tutors. Communication technologies offer the potential to overcome these weaknesses. In a conventional classroom it is possible not only to ask questions yourself but also to listen to other students' questions and to hear the answers. This is a powerful means of learning which does not rely on an individual conceiving all the useful questions to ask. Learners meet each other informally outside of the classroom and exchange ideas, question each other and challenge views. Computer-based learning loses this interaction. How can communication technologies replace it? There are a number of devices which can be used, such as:

- mailgroups where all the dialogue between learners and tutors is recorded so other learners can see the whole flow of the argument and not simply the final answer
- peer-to-peer conversations in chat rooms
- lists of frequently asked questions.

Experience of learners' use of communication technologies such as mailgroups and conferences shows that only a small minority takes part by sending messages or asking questions. A larger proportion reads the messages without making a personal contribution. This may seem a poor result, but if we consider conventional classrooms then a majority of students also do not ask questions. Although in both online and classroom situations many learners do not ask questions they do hear or read the questions and answers which is beneficial in both cases. This form of learning is called vicarious in online situations.

In a small group, most tutors aim to involve everyone, but as the size of group grows this becomes more difficult. An online tutor can encourage discussion, interaction and participation and this is largely unconnected or uninfluenced by the size of the group. Nevertheless communication technologies are not simply a way of overcoming the limitations of distance learning. Simply giving learners access to communication technologies is not a way of gaining full participation, in much the same way that putting people in a room together does not guarantee successful communication.

Summary of key points

General issues

- Online learning covers a range of approaches.
- Learners may wish to study materials on the screen and print them out so they must be designed to suit both the screen and paper.
- Designers should assume a range of technology (for example, low-speed modems) is being used and that learners may not have broadband links.
- Speed of access and movement between pages is critical to learners' interest in the material.

Structure of a website

- Design a structure which relates to the nature of the subject being studied.
- An overall design metaphor which the learners understand can aid navigation and understanding of the structure.

Links

- Wach link must have a clear purpose relative to the learning objectives.
- Links can combine any form of information and media.
- Learners are often confused about where a link has taken them (for example, to another page or within the same page).

Page layout

- Limit webpages to no more than four screen lengths.
- Present pages with a clear structure to aid learners' navigation and avoid confusion. Consistency is very important.
- Avoid pages which do not lead anywhere.

Lost in hyperspace

- Learners and other users of hypertext and hypermedia systems often complain of getting lost.
- To avoid learners feeling disoriented, structure should be straightforward, consistent and predictable.
- Overview maps and similar devices help learners to understand the structure.

Communication technologies

- Communication technologies remove the feeling of isolation which many distance learners experience. Support can be provided quickly and effectively.

Vicarious learning

- Learners benefit from access to dialogue between other students and tutors in a similar way to hearing the answer to someone else's question.

Chapter 10

Screen layout

By the end of this chapter you will have been introduced to:

- content of learning materials
- metaphors
- positioning of information
- balance of the display
- grouping
- complexity
- coding
- windows
- templates/style guides.

Content of computer-based learning materials

Always express what you aim to achieve by giving a series of learning objectives, stating what you want the learners to be able to do and understand after they have studied the package. If your material relates to the achievement of a qualification, you will have an external syllabus to satisfy. The syllabus will provide you with a statement of content which you may be tempted to use in place of your own analysis. However, it is critical that you carry out your own analysis of the subject. Designing material in the order of the presentation of the syllabus may be acceptable on some occasions, but remember your goal is to produce a high quality learning experience not to define a syllabus.

The nature of the subject must be considered before any design work is undertaken. Consider the order in which the different chunks of information should be displayed and the relationship between them. In some cases, a learner must be made aware of one piece of information in order to understand another. The sequence, links and importance of each chunk of information need to be considered before the design is developed.

All types of open learning material should contain similar features in order to aid learning; however, the delivery of these elements depends on the medium. Many of the following elements apply to all types of open or distance learning material:

1. Information to learners
   Learners must be presented with:

   - a clear statement for whom the material is designed
   - a list of what they will be able to do and understand after studying the material
   - how the material relates to qualifications or other packages
   - an explanation of how the material is structured, what support is available and how they access the support.

2. Assessment
   The learning material should ideally contain:

   - pre-tests and post-tests to help the learners understand where they start and finish after studying the package. The results of a pre-test could be used to automatically customize the material in line with the learners' achievement
   - assessment activities to provide a balance of reflection, reinforcement, self-assessment and activity where learners judge their own progress, reflect on their previous experience in comparison with the new content, reinforce their learning and be actively involved in the learning.

3. Learning content should be:

   - motivating and interesting
   - learner-centred
   - able to communicate to learners in their own language
   - able to maximize choice of what and how the learners are able to study
   - presented in small logical chunks appropriate to the subject and the learners.

4. Presentation should exploit the media to provide an interesting and effective learning environment by integrating the appropriate elements together (for example, text, graphics – realistic/logical/analogical – colour, sound, video and animation). However, effective learning is about appropriate use, not about maximizing the number of different elements you can combine together.

Screen elements

A display of computer-based learning consists of a variety of elements:

- location and navigation information
- controls
- tutorial information

- assessment
- messages (for example, feedback).

The different elements should be presented consistently and effectively throughout the entire package. Learners must know where they are in the material and how to move to other parts of the package. This can be displayed in a number of ways including:

- page numbers
- titles
- module and section names or numbers.

Control mechanisms maximize the learners' options to select where they move to next. In practice, there are often more control choices than can easily be shown. Some key options are:

- next page/frame
- back one page/frame
- main menu
- module menu
- exit.

Other possible options are:

- help
- self-assessment tests
- note taking
- glossary
- further reading
- map of the structure
- index
- search engine.

The positions of tutorial, assessment and feedback on the screen need to be defined so that learners know the purpose of anything which appears in particular areas, thus avoiding confusion and to some extent reinforcing the information. Figure 10.1 shows an example of screen element layout.

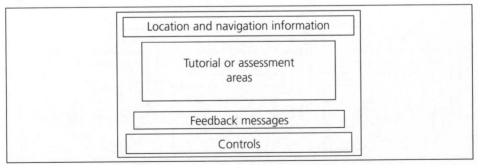

Figure 10.1   **Screen elements**

Metaphors

The following metaphors are used to design computer-based learning:

- frames
- cards
- pages.

Metaphors provide a framework for describing the design of learning materials. Computer-based training (CBT) materials are sometimes described in terms of a series of frames. Frames are displays of single screens. CBT is essentially a series of frames linked together. This is an effective way of presenting CBT but it is limited in that the computer screen is not a static environment; it is dynamic.

Early hypertext systems often used the metaphor of a card in which links were made between individual and groups of cards that contained information in the form of text and graphics. Again, this did not allow for the dynamic nature of the computer but was a useful way of helping designers to communicate about their work. Typically, the systems were centred around a home card with the material arranged in groups (or stacks) of cards which allowed the package to be modularized. A card was usually smaller than a single screen display. Figure 10.2 illustrates a simple card system.

The page metaphor has developed with the growth of the World Wide Web. One way of producing computer-based learning materials is to design material to be viewed through a browser so that the interface and page structure is standard. Since the World Wide Web is a hypertext environment, the page metaphor, like the cards is one linked to hypertext systems. Prior to the development of the World Wide Web, the page as part of a book metaphor was often used. In this situation the page was frequently limited to the size of the screen.

The frame metaphor is associated with computer-based training. The design of

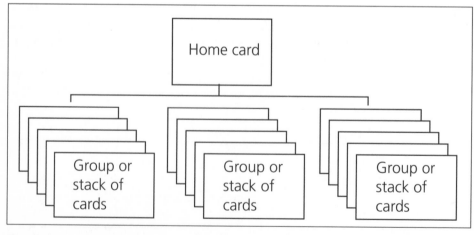

Figure 10.2   Card system

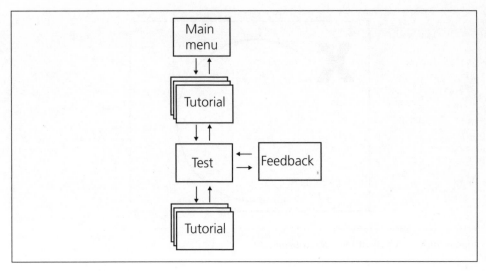

Figure 10.3   Frames

the material is described in different types of frame, each the size of a single screen of information. Standard frames are developed for tasks such as displaying tutorial information, assessment, feedback, menus and remedial help. These are combined to form the learning material. The overall structure is similar to a flow chart. Figure 10.3 illustrates a simple frame-based system.

All these approaches are useful ways of designing and describing learning materials but have limits. For example, frames and cards do not allow for the dynamic nature of the computer display, while a page does not have a defined length. It is possible to have a page which would be better described as a roll of paper rather than a single sheet.

Positioning of information

When learners view a computer display, they tend to look initially at the top left-hand corner of the screen and then work their way around the display in a clockwise direction (see Figure 10.4), probably because Western languages are read from left to right and top to bottom. If this is correct this approach to layout will fail in cultures that read in different sequences. It is possible to disrupt the cycle by employing attention-gathering methods such as colour, flashing objects, graphics and multimedia. Designers can build on this natural tendency to view the screen by positioning the information to correspond to the cycle.

Place what you want your learners to see first in the top lefthand corner. This could be the title of the material, location clues (for example, page or module number) or a motivational image. Equally, what you would like them to see last

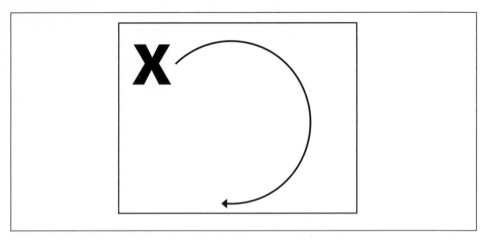

Figure 10.4   Cycle of viewing information

should be placed in the bottom lefthand corner. The learning content is placed between these two extremes.

The same reasoning can be further extended to suggest that certain areas of the screen are viewed in preference to others. This would indicate that the top half of the screen will be viewed before attention is paid to the bottom of the display. These are generalizations and simple guidelines. Other factors need to be considered, such as attentional devices, grouping information and a scrolling interface. Online materials are frequently developed around the concept of a page so that the display scrolls and the top and other areas of the display are constantly changing. You need to lay out your content to reflect its importance to the learner and subject.

Balance of the display

The overall aim of any display of computer-based learning whether it is a frame, a card or a page is to produce a clear, straightforward, interesting and consistent layout. This will aid learning by making it easy to locate information, avoid confusing the learners and motivate them to continue to studying the material. How do you achieve these objectives? One way is to produce a visual image which is balanced and predictable by using devices such as colour and graphics in a consistent and meaningful way. The value of white space is often overlooked. It can be used to balance the look of the display by separating the different areas which make up the layout. Figure 10.5 shows a comparison of a balanced and unbalanced display.

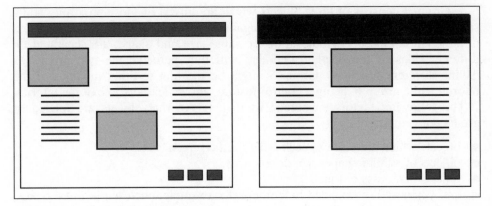

Figure 10.5   Balance of a display

Grouping of information

An organized display of material is perceived, understood and remembered better than a disorganized one. This fact would seem fairly obvious but it is easy to forget when you are under the pressure of producing materials against a deadline.

The key to an organized display is the grouping of the different screen objects. Figure 10.6 shows six different groups or chunks of information. Group 1 is perceived as a chunk since each object is a similar shape and size as well as occupying the same area of the screen. Group 2 is spread across the top of the entire display but the units are linked together by being enclosed in a rectangular

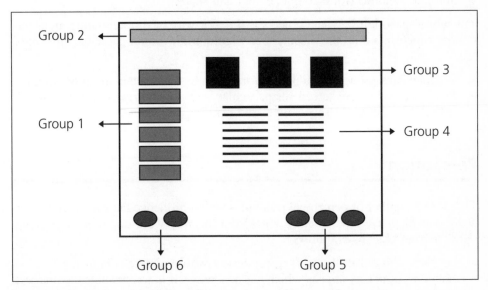

Figure 10.6   Grouping of information

box. Group 3 consists of three objects which are linked by close proximity and a similar shape. Shape, size and location again bring group 4 together. Groups 5 and 6, although composed of objects of the same size and shape, are separated on different sides of the display. Learners will thus perceive the two groups as having different functions. Group 5 might be the link to other modules of the tutorial while group 6, being a control feature, allows learners to exit the tutorial.

The following factors encourage us to perceive that objects are related or grouped together:

- objects which are close to each other on the screen
- objects of similar shape, size or colour
- objects that cross or touch
- areas enclosed or bounded by borders (for example, enclosed in lines, boxes, circles or linked by colour).

This grouping or dividing the display into chunks is important in that it can be more easily assimilated. The various components of the display can be identified, so controls, options and different parts of the learning content are easy to locate and use. Grouping or chunking items together aids readability and helps users understand the relationship between items. Grouping can be achieved in a variety of ways. The most frequently used techniques are:

- colour coding
- enclosing groups within a box
- proximity (that is, objects which are close together)
- highlighting
- similar shapes of objects
- multiple methods (for example, colour and shape).

The white space left between objects is a major way of differentiating areas and groups which make up the display (see Figure 10.6). Some guidelines to follow are:

- Separate each group or chunk of information by 3 to 5 blank rows or columns.
- Reserve areas of the screen for particular types of information (for example, commands, status messages, input and warning messages).

Perception

There are a number of perceptual principles which influence the way learners perceive a display. We have already considered the way we group objects together. Other perceptions are as follows:

- Learners will fill in the gaps to produce a whole picture (Figure 10.7 shows examples of partial objects which learners may fill in to complete the images).
- Perception depends on the learners' experience (that is, they will compare

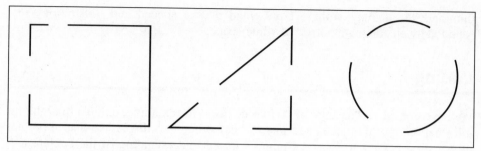

Figure 10.7   Filling the gaps

    images with their previous knowledge in order to understand them. This can be either a powerful way of reinforcing an experience or a source of confusion).

- Learners will see a relationship between objects which are physically close to each other.
- Learners prefer balance in a display.
- Objects that are enclosed by a border or are part of a symmetrical display will be seen as related.
- Learners tend to see what they expect to see (for example, they will fill in a missing word in a text).

Complexity

Screen layout is influenced by two key factors:

- the grouping or chunking of information, and
- the complexity of the overall display.

We have already considered the nature of grouping information. When considering complexity you should avoid putting too much information on a single-screen display. A display should use only a minority (approximately 30 per cent) of the screen. The majority of the screen should be left blank. This allows learners to locate and study the key information. In a complex display, it is very easy for learners to miss important items in the overall mass of information. You can partly alleviate this by using methods such as grouping or colour coding of information but it is preferable to avoid designing complex and over-dense displays in the first place.

    An effective method of limiting complexity is to focus on a learning objective in each display. Only information related to this single objective should be included. This focus not only reduces complexity, but it is also good learning practice in that it avoids confusing the learners with peripheral information.

    The best advice is to keep the display straightforward and simple with a clear unambiguous structure. The order of the information should be obvious to the learners who have their attention drawn to the key points. White space should dominate the display with text presented double spaced and illustrations surrounded by an adequate border of white space.

Coding

We have considered a range of coding devices (for example, colour) to highlight information, group objects, add interest and structure a display so that important information is easy to locate. Coding will aid understanding of the content and thus learning. Although it is perfectly possible to use a single means of coding a display, it is often more effective to combine different methods. This reinforces the message (Figure 10.8 combines graphical elements, shading and text). However, the different methods must reinforce each other and not contradict, otherwise it will confuse learners.

| Heading | Page 1 of 6 |

| Heading | Page 1 of 6 |

Figure 10.8   Combining different coding methods

Learners have different learning styles and preferences. Some prefer information in the form of words, either printed or verbal, while others prefer visual content. The degree of preference varies considerably. Learning material must provide for learners with all combinations of preferences.

Consideration of the use of coding devices to reinforce messages with the need to cater for different learners' preferences suggests that we must combine different methods and at the same time avoid a confusing and distracting display.

Table 10.1 compares the different methods and judges their suitability to reinforce each other.

Windows

Most modern operating systems and applications employ windows as their main method of presentation. A window is a rectangular area in which information can be displayed. The size of windows can be changed by users so that many windows can be displayed at the same time although normally only one is active (that is, the focus of the users' attention and work). The overwhelming use of windows in computing suggests that it should also be adopted for computer-based learning materials, assuming that your learners are regular computer users. Clearly this is not always the case.

Table 10.1   *Comparison of coding methods*

Method	Combinations	Comments
Text: ● size ● style ● bold ● italics	Both colour and graphics can be combined effectively with text and each other. They must reinforce each other and care should be taken to avoid clashes.	All the different text approaches are useful provided that they are employed consistently and not excessively. Remember that screen resolution makes text quality poor compared to print on a page.
Colour: ● blinking ● reverse video	Blinking and reverse video are useful attentional devices combined with text. Do not use together. Colour is probably more effective than either of them.	Limited use of colour is very effective in reinforcing text and graphics in all forms. Overuse will confuse, distract and irritate learners.
Graphics: ● shapes ● lines (thickness)	Simple use of graphic features such as underlining headings or dividing the display are very effective. Enclosing areas of the display forms groups which helps learners identify relationships.	The computer screen is an excellent environment for graphics. They can add structure, enhance meaning and replace text.

Windows has developed into the dominant presentation method because of a variety of factors, including:

● being able to work on more than one set of information at a time
● operating on more than one application at a time
● integrating a range of tasks together.

The intention is to provide you with a computer environment which helps you deal with a complex and busy world. Do learners have the same need when working on computer-based learning materials? Normally, designers are trying to avoid distracting and confusing learners while allowing them to concentrate on the critical points of the material. These are not the same objectives as a windows environment.

Although there is this difference in objectives, you should not dismiss windows entirely. They can serve many useful purposes in computer-based learning without compromising the basic approach of simplicity, clarity and order. Windows can provide learners with:

● comparisons (for example, output from a simulation can be shown in one window as a graph and in another as numerical data)
● additional or more advanced information on a topic by overlaying the original display with a window
● context-sensitive help while maintaining the original display
● feedback in an overlaying window
● a note-taking facility
● extra information to an illustration (for example, clicking on different parts of a diagram opens a window explaining that element)

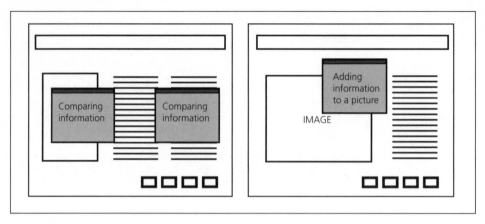

Figure 10.9   Using windows

- comparison of information from several sources (for example, historic documents, video sequences and so on). This would allow a subject to be explored and studied in detail.

Figure 10.9 shows windows being used to compare information and to add information to an illustration.

As with other features of computer-based learning, it is important to use windows in a consistent, systematic and limited way. The overuse of windows is likely to confuse learners, reduce the learning value and produce a negative effect. Windows are a device more suitable for computer literate learners. If the learners are new or non-computer users, then windows are probably unsuitable.

As a designer of learning material, you have the choice of allowing your windows to maintain their dynamic features of motion, changing size and shape, and opening and closing. These important features add considerable value to their use but again they do require learners who understand how to manipulate windows. You could, however, use fixed size windows which can only be open and closed.

It is easy to become confused when interacting with a number of windows because overlapping windows hide each other. Figure 10.10 illustrates this problem. You can design windows which do not completely hide each other, thus avoiding the problem of confusing your learners, but it is at the expense of limiting the maximum size of the window.

Guidelines for the use of windows in computer-based learning materials depend to some extent on the learners' computer experience. However, some guidelines are:

- Limit the number of windows displayed to no more than two at any one time.
- Consider the dynamic nature of windows in relation to the purpose they are serving (for example, learners probably need to move and change windows if they are comparing different information or if an extra application such as a

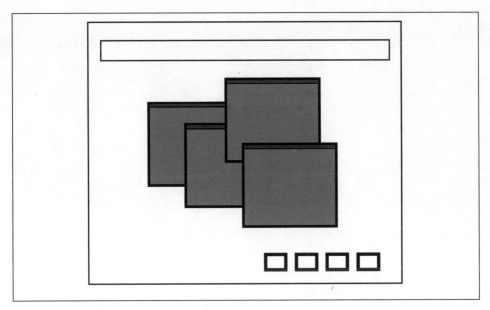

Figure 10.10   Overlapping windows

note-taking is being provided, but windows used to add information to an illustration could be fixed).
● Design windows which cannot completely hide each other.
● Standardize windows (for example, the headings, buttons and borders) to avoid confusion in manipulating them.

There is another form of windows called tiled. Tiled windows are used on a far more limited scale than dynamic windows. They expand or contract to fill the available space. A single tiled window will fill the entire screen, two will occupy half the display each, four a quarter and so on. The user can adjust the size of a tiled window and the remainder contract or expand to compensate. Tiled windows are regarded as less confusing for a user with limited computer experience, but a display with several tiled windows is very complex and potentially difficult to understand or locate information. Subsequently, tiled windows are not often used in computer-based learning materials.

Templates/style guides

Designing computer-based learning involves the combination of many different factors to produce an effective learning environment. Many organizations have developed standard templates or detailed style guides ensuring that a consistent approach and quality standards are maintained. These methods have the additional

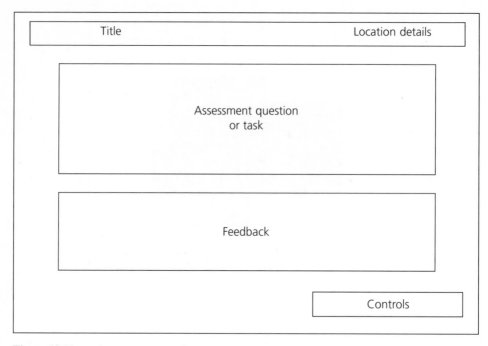

Figure 10.11   Assessment template

benefit of providing a distinct 'look and feel' to all the products produced. Learners will become familiar with the controls, structure and format and therefore should find the material straightforward to use. However, there is the danger of familiarity breeding contempt. Learners can become bored with seeing the same structure. This problem can be overcome by providing a range of templates and allowing some freedom to the designer.

Templates designed for standard computer-based learning functions include:

- presenting information (text only)
- presenting information (text and graphics)
- assessment (reflective, reinforcement and action)
- feedback
- main menu
- section menu.

Figure 10.11 shows an example of an assessment template.

Style guides explain the presentation and interaction of the user interface. They detail the use of colour, design of communication styles (for example, menus), presentation of information, attentional devices, use of illustrations and all other aspects of the interface. Style guides aid consistency between products but can be limiting in that design freedom is restricted. They are used widely in designing computer applications such as word-processors, spreadsheets and databases.

Summary of key points

Content

- Computer-based learning material should provide information, assessment and learning content.

Screen elements

- The main screen elements are location, navigation, controls, assessment and messages.

Metaphors

- Metaphors provide learners with a structure which helps them to understand the learning material.
- Frames, cards and pages are three metaphors which have been widely used.

Position of information

- Learners who use Western languages will tend to look initially at the top left-hand corner and then move in a clockwise direction around the screen.

Perceptual issues

- Learners prefer a balanced display.
- Grouping allows learners to perceive, understand and remember the information displayed.
- Grouping can be achieved by position, shape, colour, size, location and by being enclosed.
- Learners tend to see what they expect to see so they will fill in the gaps in geometrical shapes or insert missing words in sentences.
- Displays should avoid complexity by using only about 30 per cent of the available space.
- Information should be highlighted by using multiple coding methods such as colour and graphics.

Windows

- Although windows are a powerful means of presenting information they should be used with care in computer-based learning to avoid confusing new computer users.
- They should be limited to no more than two at a time, relate to the learning purpose, be designed so that they do not hide each other and provide standard features.

Templates

- Templates and style guides provide a means of ensuring a consistent standard approach but do limit design freedom to some extent.

Chapter 11

Content

By the end of this chapter you will have been introduced to:

- different types of content
- scripting process
- storyboarding
- the methods of information collection
- learning styles and strategies
- design teams
- illustrations
- chunking
- copyright
- proof reading.

In many discussions about designing learning materials the emphasis is on the presentation, interaction and technology. Rarely is the content of the material considered, which is surprising since from the learners' point of view that is the whole point of studying the package. This lack of interest can result in attractive and engaging computer-based learning materials which are, essentially, free of content.

Content is located in a variety of forms, including:

- examples
- descriptions and explanations
- case studies
- assessment – tests, questions and other forms
- good practice
- practical short cuts and solutions to problems
- sequence of presentation
- ideas and concepts

- theories
- references
- rules, standards, guidelines and principles associated with the subject
- relationships between different elements
- algorithms, tables, graphs and charts
- pictures, graphics and slide shows
- video.

Content is not simply information that you can locate in a book, view on a video or hear on a cassette. It requires the expertise of practitioners to be extracted and analysis of current practice to be undertaken. When developing computer-based learning it is easy to concentrate on design and not give content the attention it deserves. It is vital that content is gathered systematically, employing a design team member who understands the subject so that the key information is identified and the value of new ideas is appreciated.

Scripting

In a commercial development your customer may provide you with a specification and possibly a needs assessment. However, the degree of detail provided is often very limited so that early in a project you will need to develop a script of the content. A useful way to begin is with a brainstorm or a series of them to identify what could be included in the learning material. This provides a starting point with the specification and needs analysis to develop a script or storyboard for the material. Figure 11.1 illustrates the steps and shows the roles of analysing and evaluating play.

Scripting is an iterative process so you are continuously developing, enhancing and changing it until you are satisfied that it meets the needs of the project. The content you have created or sourced is analysed by the team (probably by the subject and learning experts) and evaluated by typical learners and other experts. Their feedback then influences the script and subsequently the content. This is a creative process and the number of loops required will depend on the individual project. It may take two or ten. The more iterations the higher the cost, so the overall project manager needs to ensure that each loop is necessary.

A key element of the script is a series of learning objectives or outcomes which define what learners will achieve by studying the material. These objectives will essentially provide you clear guidance about the nature and content of the computer-based learning material. Scripts can take a variety of forms, such as:

- a full narrative description of each learning objective broken down into its component parts
- a list of the key points related to each objective
- a storyboard of the whole or part of the material.

The degree of detail and nature of the script depends on both the preferences of

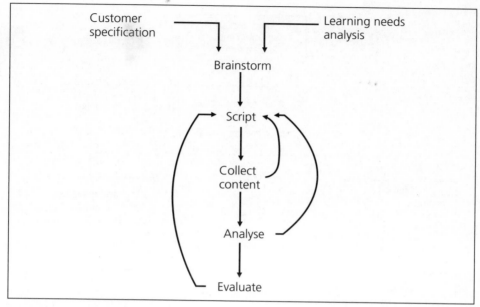

Figure 11.1   Scripting process

the team, the customer and nature of the task. A large design team may find a more detailed script useful to ensure consistency and aid communication within the group. If you are working for a client they may wish to review the content before agreeing to implement it, so a detailed script will be needed.

Example: Basic Script Approach
1. Mentoring
2. Enrolment and password systems
3. Module 1: Introduction
   ● What outcomes can the learner expect from studying the material?
   ● How to make the best use of computer-based learning
   ● Study advice.
4. Links to:
   ● What is mentoring and pre-test modules
5. Media
   ● audio – voice over
   ● still images.

Storyboarding

One approach to scripting is to develop a storyboard, a visual representation which illustrates the content, navigation and structure of the learning materials. Figure 11.2 illustrates part of an overview storyboard for a mentoring package, showing

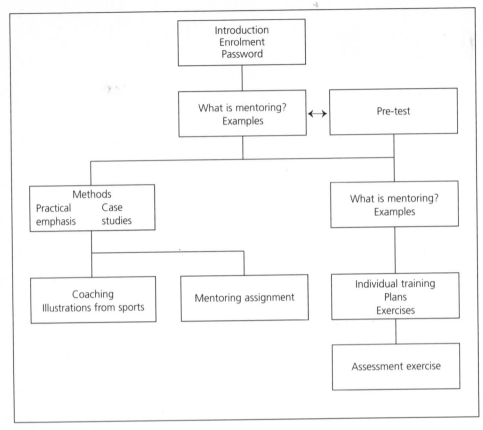

Figure 11.2   Storyboard

some of the modules of the material with suggestions for what will happen in that module (for example, exercise and assignments).

Storyboards can be developed to show each screen display or simply remain as an overview of the major elements of the material, depending on what you want to achieve. They have a very useful additional function in that they are a straightforward way of describing the content of the material to the whole team, customers and other stakeholders. It is important to avoid confusion and duplication of effort where a number of people are designing the modules.

Methods of collecting information

Designers use a variety of methods to collect content information.

Outlining

The initial step in identifying the content of the material requires the scope of project to be outlined. It is best to start by listing or drawing a chart of all the areas which might be relevant to the development. Figure 11.3 shows a spider chart of subjects relating to a learning package on mentoring. It is only partially completed but provides the essence of the concept.

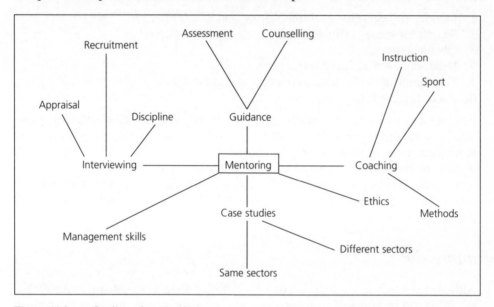

Figure 11.3   Outline of mentoring

At the start of the project it is best to consider everything that might possibly be relevant. During the process of analysing, reviewing and evaluating, the material will be narrowed and focused until it directly supports the learning objectives (see Figure 11.4).

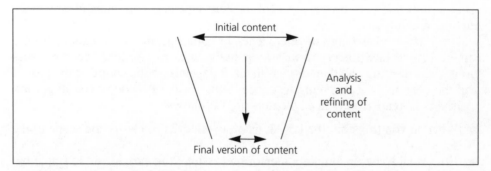

Figure 11.4   Reviewing the content

Literature review

In almost all projects it is useful to review the published sources relevant to your subject, including not only the printed material (books, journals and reports) but also videos, audio sources and online content. This requires a search of the literature in libraries and online (World Wide Web). The early listing of subjects which might be suitable for the project is useful in that it provides an idea of items to search for. The process of a subject review is:

1. Identify subjects (for example, listing and spider charts).
2. Search for sources (for example, library and online).
3. Obtain sources.
4. Read, review and analyse material.
5. Take notes of useful ideas, concepts and approaches.
6. Record references.

Reading a range of books, articles and reports may take many weeks. It is therefore important to take good notes so that the value of the investment is maximized. A frequent error is not to record the source of your notes. In many cases you will want to refer back to the source later in the project or to acknowledge them or to seek permission to use some of their material. During this process it is relatively easy to develop an excellent bibliography which can be included in the learning package.

Interviews

Although published material can be very helpful, there is no substitute for gathering information yourself from experts or other people with relevant experience. They can provide the context for the subject, identify the key issues and illustrate the practical problems. It is therefore important to talk to the people with experience. Interviews can be an individual or group action but in both cases need to be systematically and professionally undertaken.

You may have very clear objectives for the interview, such as to gather examples and small case studies, but it is usually wise to elicit their widest views. This ensures that your own analysis of the core subject is correct and that you are missing nothing vital.

There are a wide range of approaches to gathering this information, from a simple face-to-face interview to asking individuals to consider specific issues prior to the meeting and then discuss them. It depends on the nature of the project and the content you are trying to create. Some of the questions you might ask managers who are experienced mentors are as follows:

- What do you think are the key skills of a mentor? (To clarify the scope of the subject.)
- How would you undertake a mentoring session? (To provide an example but also to identify any gaps in current practice.)

- How long does it take for mentoring to start to show progress? (To identify time scales.)
- Could you give any examples where you feel mentoring worked well and why? (To identify good examples.)
- Could you give examples where you feel mentoring failed and why? (To identify bad examples.)
- What would you include in the package? (To check that the content is correct.)

Interviews or discussions with potential learners provide guidance on appropriate language, terms and approaches. It is vital that the finished material is refined to meet the requirements of the target audience.

In the sample questions we concentrated on the mentor, but it would also be useful to ask similar questions of the learners in order to gain their perspective.

A group discussion could follow this type of individual interview where a summary of interviews is given to the group. This would allow a debate on the issues to take place to ensure that everyone agrees with your conclusions. New ideas, examples and approaches often emerge from the interaction of the group. You could ask one person to make notes of the discussion while another facilitates the meeting.

Questionnaires

Interviews are effective but generally time consuming and limited to a relatively small number. If you are interested in gathering the views of a large group of people then you need to use a questionnaire. These are an efficient way of gathering information provided they are carefully designed and limited. It is best to concentrate on one or two main issues so that the questionnaire is not over-long (no more than three sides of A4 paper) and encourages participants to complete it. It is not unusual for only a minority of the questionnaires to be returned completed (a 20 per cent return is good for a public postal questionnaire). Within a closed community of an individual organization better returns can be achieved by asking senior managers to endorse the questionnaire, but even in that case a return of 66 per cent would be excellent.

It is good practice to pilot a questionnaire with a small group before sending it out, to ensure that it is not misleading or ambiguous. A sample of half a dozen can provide valuable feedback on a questionnaire to ensure it is effective.

Observation

If you are developing a computer-based learning package on a practical topic it is always worth visiting the locations of the work and observing the tasks being undertaken. This provides you with the opportunity to gain an insight into the context of the subject so that the material is realistic and relevant. Observation can help you to check if the learning material is accurate. During a visit, photographs or video film can be taken which provide a realistic look and feel to your material. However, learners tend to expect high quality images and film so a professional photographer is not a luxury but a necessity.

If you plan to observe people undertaking tasks or to photograph them it is essential to seek their personal permission as well as that of the organization. Many people are reluctant to be watched.

Learning styles and strategies

Everyone has different preferences about how and what they like to learn. These are called learning styles. There are several ways of defining learning styles. The main point for designing learning material and creating content is to ensure that you provide a number of alternative explanations and approaches to each topic. Some people prefer a highly visual presentation of information while others are content with a narrative description. So avoid being too narrow, offer choice to the learners and create content which can be used flexibly.

Most learners also have distinct learning strategies which they will want to employ on your material. If you involve typical learners as part of the design approach then you will become familiar with their preferences and can include these strategies into your design. Some general issues relating to strategies which many learners will find helpful are as follows:

- Minimize the stress of studying.
- Explain the relevance of a content to them.
- Review the learning material frequently.
- Break the subject into discrete items of learning.
- Practice.
- Feedback on performance.

Tutors and trainers

Conventional tutors and trainers of the subject can offer you a unique insight since they are aware of the learners' reaction to each aspect of the topic. They have a wealth of practical experience in explaining the various ideas through conventional methods of presentation, practical exercise and discussion. An experienced tutor is able to tell you:

- the ideas learners find most difficult and how they overcome these difficulties
- what order to present the content in to ensure the most effective results
- how to structure exercises to gain the most effect
- the typical questions learners want answered
- the typical misconceptions learners have

- what learners find most straightforward
- what typical learners already know and understand about the subject.

Tutors and trainers are key to the success of a computer-based learning development not only to help with the design but also to review and evaluate the finished product.

Design team

Design teams come in many shapes and sizes. It is rare that a single individual produces professional computer-based learning. In some case one person may provide several areas, but the following expertise is essential:

- project management
- technical expertise
- subject expertise
- learning expertise
- graphic design
- research skills
- writing skills.

It is tempting to see the development of software as the key issue but more computer-based learning fails due to poor learning design and/or content than to technical problems, although some do. Subject and learning design expertise are vital requisites.

Chunking

Computer-based learning is quite restrictive about the amount of information that can be effectively presented on a single screen. It is also good practice to break learning materials into small chunks since learners find these easier to assimilate. These two factors suggest that as you are developing content it is sound practice to divide content into small sections with related illustrations, examples, interactions and assessments. It is a reasonable rule of thumb to limit each display to a single idea or concept and to present and relate only information which is relevant to that concept.

Illustrations

Illustrations are important to computer-based learning because it is a medium which is not ideal for the display of text. An image has the potential to be a powerful means of communicating with learners. In terms of content there are a variety of images you might wish to create or obtain, including:

- graphic images – representative, analogical and logical
- real photographs
- video.

There are considerable volumes of images already available in the forms of libraries of clip art, CD-ROMs of photographs and even a range of short video sequences. You therefore have the choice of buying images or creating them. The cost of creating new images is high but you do gain the benefits of illustrations which meet your precise needs and in which you have the copyright since you created them. Clip art is available in very large volumes but to identify suitable illustrations can necessitate you viewing hundreds and perhaps thousands of images. When you buy collections of images it is vital to check the restrictions placed on their use by the copyright holder. Images may frequently be used for non-commercial purposes only.

Still photographs are relatively easy to take with digital cameras. However, high quality is required by learners so you may want to commission a professional photographer.

Obtaining video sequences to meet precise needs is very difficult and in most cases you will need new video for your package. Video is both expensive and time consuming to produce. You should always carefully assess your reasons for having video, or whether a series of still images can serve the same purpose.

Copyright

It is probably best to assume that all content is subject to copyright so that collecting existing material for your package is not going to be simple. Always consider the ownership of all the material. The conditions that the copyright holder places on the content vary from 'free to copy as long as source is acknowledged' to 'no form of copying is permitted'. You must check the conditions that apply and seek permission to use the content. Permission will not always be granted and in many cases a fee will be charged. It can take a long time to gain permission so start early.

Proof reading

Frequent problems with all forms of computer-based learning are spelling and grammatical errors. It only takes a few mistakes to present a poor image of the product to the learners. Well-motivated learners are vital to the success of all types of learning. If they gain the impression that the material has been poorly developed or done in a rush their interest and attention is potentially going to be damaged. It is important to systematically proof read the final version of the learning material to ensure the highest quality of product. Your aim is to present material with no errors.

Spelling and grammatical checkers are useful in helping to minimize mistakes (remember to check on UK and USA differences). However, they do not replace a human reviewer who can read every line and identify the errors which the electronic checks will miss. Proof reading requires concentration and is very tiring so it should be undertaken by several people working in short shifts to maximize their efficiency. They are searching for:

- spelling mistakes
- poor grammar
- duplications
- inconsistencies
- poor presentation.

Summary of key points

General issues

- From the learners' point of view the content is the whole point of studying the package.
- Content takes a wide variety of forms.
- Content must be systematically gathered by the design team in order to identify the key information and new ideas.

Scripting

- A script is useful in helping to identify the required content.
- Scripting is an iterative process.
- A vital element of the script is the learning objectives or outcomes which define what learners will achieve by studying the material.
- The degree of detail and nature of the script depends on the preferences of the team, customer and nature of the task.

Storyboarding

- A storyboard is essentially a visual representation which illustrates the content, navigation and structure of the learning materials.
- Storyboards can be developed to show each screen display or simply remain as an overview of the major elements of the material.

Methods of collecting information

- The initial step in identifying the content of the material requires the scope of project to be outlined. A spider chart can be a useful way of presenting the scope.
- Review the published sources (for example, books, journals, reports, videos, audio and online) to identify content, ideas and approaches.
- Interviewing can help with gathering information from experts or other people with relevant experience.
- Questionnaires can help with gathering information from a large group of people with relevant experience.
- Visit the locations of the work and observe the tasks being undertaken. This provides you with an insight into the context of the subject so that the material is realistic and relevant.

Learning styles and strategies

- Create content which allows the learner choice and flexibility.

Tutors and trainers

- Subject tutors and trainers can offer a unique insight. They are aware of the learners' reaction to each aspect of the topic.

Design team

- Design teams come in a wide range of shapes and sizes.

Chunking

- Divide content into small sections with related illustrations, examples, interactions and assessments.

Illustrations

- The key choice is between creating or buying illustrations.

Proofreading

● It is vital to proof read the content.

Copyright

● You must check the copyright of all content and seek permission to use the material when it is required.

Chapter 12

Evaluation

By the end of this chapter you will have been introduced to:

- formative and summative evaluation
- field trials and cost effectiveness
- evaluation methods, such as learner and expert reviews, observation, speak aloud protocols, interviews and questionnaires
- standards and checklists.

What is evaluation?

Evaluation can take a variety of forms but is mainly concerned with improving the quality of the computer-based learning material. It can do this in many ways including:

- organizing the systematic testing of the material with users and other stake-holders (for example, managers, trainers and tutors)
- comparing the objectives of the project with the outcomes achieved
- using subject experts to review the material.

Formative evaluation is undertaken during the development process to ensure that the work benefits from feedback from the users and other experts. This evaluation process can take place at any point during the life of the project. It is often helpful to integrate formative evaluation into the project plan so that each stage of development is able to access high quality feedback.

Field trials are a useful method of formative evaluation in that the material is tested with the target group of learners in their natural environment. Excellent results can be obtained with relatively small numbers of learners so that groups of less than ten can often be sufficient. It is important to realize that learners will be able to give you powerful feedback concerning issues such as:

- readability
- presentation
- motivation
- navigation.

However, they will not be able to help with ensuring the material is correct or complete and you will need to include a subject matter expert to check these points. A field trial should include methods such as observation, questionnaires and interviews to gather the learners' responses to the material.

In contrast to field trials is summative evaluation which covers the whole project once it is completed. The original objectives of the development are compared with the outcome to judge the overall degree of success and to decide if the project was effective. A key element in summative evaluation is to judge the cost effectiveness of the development. This is not simply about calculating the costs but about comparing the benefits of the computer-based learning materials with a another approach to solving the same learning need. Benefits are not only financial but take all forms. The outcomes of summative evaluations often influence the design of any further new versions of the package.

Computer-based learning materials are not only learning materials, they are also software, and an important part of any evaluation is to ensure that the product functions effectively as a computer application. This evaluation follows a similar pattern to that of the content. It should involve learners and experts, contribute feedback during the creation of the product and also take place at the end of the project. It is vital for the credibility of the material that it is free of errors and easy to install and use, all of which require systematic testing at all stages of the project.

Methods

There are various methods which can be employed to evaluate or test computer-based learning materials. Many of them are similar to those that you can use to identify content (for example, questionnaires). A key resource is learner feedback throughout the development process. Learners need to be involved at all stages, from the initial scoping of the product to the final sign off.

Learner feedback

To be successful, learning material should motivate the learners. The only way of ensuring that material is motivating is to involve learners in its creation. Learners' evaluation is vital and should be integrated into all steps of the development. It is therefore useful to ask learners what they think about initial design ideas or even to involve them in brainstorming sessions to identify possible approaches. Some key points on which to seek learner comments are:

- initial design ideas – sketches of interfaces, choice of metaphors and learning outcomes/objectives
- design guidelines
- first software prototypes
- field trials of individual modules
- field trials of the whole package
- final software prototypes.

One approach that has proved useful is to involve a small group of learners throughout the development. These learners work with the design team which allows them to gain a detailed understanding of the project so that they are able to provide informed feedback to the team. However, the danger is that they identify with the design team and not with the objectives of the project so that their feedback becomes more about saying what they believe the designers want to hear than what needs to be said.

Expert reviews

Although learners can provide feedback on almost all aspects of the development, remember that they know little about the subject since they are learning about it and also that they have limited experience of the different design options available to computer-based learning materials. This probably means that you need three types of expertise:

- subject matter
- training/teaching
- design.

There are likely to be few occasions when you can combine all three in the same individual and often there is an advantage in having a range of people since this gives you broad feedback. The subject expert is able to tell you if you are comprehensively covering the topics and if any key issues are missing. The training or teaching expert can help identify if material is being presented using the best learning methods, while the design expert can suggest alternative ways of exploiting the computer medium.

Observation

Observation is an important method which can be used with both learners and experts. Anyone using the computer-based learning material can be observed to ensure their reactions and behaviour is captured. People who are concentrating on using a product are often not in a position to remember all their choices and reactions while a separate observer can offer valuable additional evidence.

The observer can be a person who simply positions him or herself to gain a clear view of the interaction while not interfering with it. However, a human observer is likely to need to take notes and it is very difficult, if not impossible, to record everything. Equally most people are conscious of being observed and this may influence their behaviour. A short session will require considerable concentration and note taking if everything is to be considered. It is probably best to use a human observer when you want to focus on a limited range of issues so that the burden of note taking and concentration is reduced.

If you wish to capture the whole interaction between the learner or expert and the system then it is probably best to use a video camera. Although a camera has the potential to record everything, in practice it is difficult for a single camera to achieve. Frequently more than one camera is required. A human observer can decide to change position or adjust their view. It is difficult to do this with a camera once it has been placed. Where two or more cameras are employed they need to be synchronized to help with later analysis.

A human observer will, to a limited extent, analyse their observations while they are undertaking the task. A video recording will need to be analysed from scratch which can be time consuming. However, a good video recording will capture a full record of the interaction while even an expert human observer will only collect a limited account.

Speak aloud

Observation can capture many things but it is unable to discover what the learners or expert are thinking about when they are making decisions. This is critical to understanding the effectiveness of the material (for example, whether the presentation is confusing so that learners make a poor choice by having to guess). One approach which can be very useful in gaining an insight into the minds of learners and experts using the learning material is speaking aloud. The users are asked to explain what they are thinking as they work through the material. Their comments are recorded so that they can be analysed later.

Although this can be a very useful method in practice few people are able to provide a complete commentary. Many are self-conscious when asked to provide comments on their actions and thoughts. It is often useful to ask learners and experts to practise on another system before undertaking the evaluation.

Computer logging

Computer-based learning packages can be rich environments offering many options and choices for the learners. It is therefore useful to evaluate the learners' choice of routes through the material and each decision that the learners make. This can only be done by using the computer itself to log every move the learner or expert makes. Computer logging can record every key press so it provides a detailed record of the interaction. Logging is obviously very useful but can take a great deal of time to analyse.

Tests

In many cases you need to test particular aspects of the system that you have created. Tests may be technical (for example, installing the learning material on a variety of different systems, networks or on a website to be downloaded) or related to the content. It may be useful to devise a standard test or set of tests for your learners or experts to use for evaluating the material.

Questionnaires

After a group of learners or experts have tried the computer-based learning material a questionnaire is often useful to capture their views. There are three main types of question that you can ask:

- structured
- semi-structured
- open.

A structured question is one where the answer is chosen from a series of options.

Example of structured question
How often have you used computer-based learning products?

1. Frequently (more than five times)
2. Occasionally (more than once but less than five times)
3. Never

Please circle your chosen option.

Structured questions are very useful to gain information that is straightforward to analyse and complete. However, the answers are fairly limited and do not allow your users to volunteer information.

An open question is one where the learners or experts are not constrained. They can answer it in any way they choose.

Example of open question
What did you like about the learning material?
....
....
....
....
....

Open questions allow you to capture the full unconstrained responses from your learners and experts. However, they are not easy to analyse.

Semi-structured questions are a mix of open and structured approaches.

Example of semi-structured question

Have you ever used computer-based learning materials before? Please circle your reply.

Yes

No

If yes, please describe your experience below:

....

....

....

In practice you would normally use a mix of types of question so that you gain a balance of easy to analyse answers while allowing learners and experts to express their opinions.

Interview

After a group of learners or experts have tried the computer-based learning material it is usual to interview them to capture their experiences. The interview can take a variety of forms in a similar way to questionnaires:

- a structured interview
- an open interview
- a mixed interview.

A structured interview involves asking each person the same questions. This provides answers which you can compare and analyse against each other. Interviewers do not require a great deal of skill to undertake a structured interview since they are simply asking standard questions and trying to record the full answers.

An open interview is one where the questions depend on the answers given. Interviewers are free to follow up answers, probe the responses and in general attempt to gain a detailed insight into the views of the interviewee. They are very powerful devices which fully capture the views of the interviewee. However, they do require skilled interviewers to carry them out and answers are difficult to analyse since they do not relate to standard questions.

A mixed interview involves asking everyone a set of standard questions but allows the interviewer to probe any answers which are interesting or just different. The mixed approach again requires a skilled interviewer but does reduce the difficulty in analysing the answers and allows a degree of detail to be captured.

Combinations of methods

Most evaluations consist of a mix of methods to ensure that the results are soundly based. You might use a questionnaire so that many learners can be included in the evaluation and then interview a small group based on the results of the questionnaire. This would provide both width and depth.

Table 12.1 shows a summary of the different methods to allow for ease of comparison.

Table 12.1   *Evaluation methods*

Methods	Strengths	Weaknesses	Notes
Learner feedback	Involvement is essential to ensure material is suitable	Limited knowledge of the content	Small number of learners can provide valuable insight
Expert reviews	Considerable knowledge of subject and learning methods	May not be representative of learners	
Questionnaires	Cover large numbers of subjects Can combine different types of questions	Relatively limited depth Response rates are often low	
Interviews	Capable of producing considerable depth	Expensive in time and in most cases limited to small numbers of subjects	Open interviewing requires expert interviewers
Computer logging	Complete record	Analysis can be lengthy	
Speak aloud	Provides an insight into subjects' thinking	Few subjects find the approach easy	
Tests	Essential for checking technical issues	Can be expensive to undertake	

Checklists

Many organizations have developed computer-based learning standards which can serve both as a means of assisting the development of material or as an approach to evaluating a finished product. Three checklists available from websites are:

- Institute of IT Training – http://www.iitt.org.uk– Standards for TBT Learning Materials
- Technologies for Training – http://www.tft.co.uk – Criteria for the Design and Evaluation of TBT Materials

- Learndirect – http://www.ufiltd.co.uk – Endorsement Criteria for Ufi Materials.

Many commercial developers of computer-based learning materials have also published guidelines, standards and checklists which are often available for downloading from their websites. In addition academic sites at universities throughout the world offer guidelines for the development of materials. These are mainly aimed at university staff developing materials for higher education but are frequently relevant to other situations.

At the start of a project it is useful to consider a range of standards, guidelines and checklists to produce a set for your own situation or to adopt one which you feel meets your needs.

The following simple checklist illustrates the issues you would want to review:

- Who are the materials suitable for?
- What will learners be able to do after studying the material?
- What will learners know after studying the material?
- What does the material assume the learners know already?
- What mixture of media does the material use (for example, video, text, sound and so on)?
- How motivating are the materials?
- How much support does the package require?

An important issue to consider in terms of computer-based learning materials is how easy the material is to install. The learning material is useless unless you can access it on a computer. The package must be designed so that installation is straightforward. Detailed installation instructions must accompany the material.

Representative samples

Evaluation is often based on analysing the evidence provided by groups of learners and other stakeholders in the development. However, this assumes that the individuals involved are typical of all the learners who will eventually use the package. It is important that everyone who takes part in an evaluation is representative of the whole population of learners. In most cases a small sample of learners can identify a large proportion of the problems within a package, but if they are not typical this may result in changes which make the package less suitable. Time spent ensuring you have a useful sample is a sound investment. The evaluation needs to compare the characteristics of the sample with whole groups of learners. Some factors to compare are:

- age
- gender
- experience of subject, skills and so on
- computer literacy

- location
- work roles.

Cost effectiveness

Cost effectiveness involves judging a variety of factors of which cost is an important, but not the only issue. You must compare other methods of meeting the learning need and indeed not undertaking any action. Consider the impact on each learner of completing the package and the overall consequences for the organization.

The comparison between computer-based learning and other methods has often been based on the time required to produce an hour of learning material. The learning hour is not a precise unit since it is based on how much material a typical learner can cover in an hour, but it does provide a reasonable comparison. Computer-based learning consists of a wide range of materials and thus the time to create each type will be different.

Table 12.2 provides an estimate of how long it will take to create different types of learning material.

Table 12.2   *Development time*

Type of learning material	Time to develop an hour of material (hours)
Classroom session	8
Basic quality linear video	20 to 50
Open learning text pack	20 to 80
Online learning (text-based material)	20 to 80
Online learning (integrated resource)	80 to 300
Computer-based learning (text, still images and graphics)	150 to 300
Computer-based learning (multimedia)	300 to 1000

The table shows that, considering development, computer-based learning is substantially more expensive to produce than other types of learning material. To balance this comparison you need to consider the benefits of computer-based learning. The important factors to review in any study of cost effectiveness include:

- number of learners – computer-based learning is more accessible than conventional methods so far more learners can access the material. You are not limited by available classrooms and tutors. Learners will not need to wait for the course so errors due to a lack of training and so on can be avoided.
- saving travel costs and time – computer-based learning can be studied at the workplace so travelling time and costs saved can be substantial where hundreds of learners are involved. Travel costs and time are often more expensive than the cost of the conventional training event.

- lost production – since learners are free to choose when they study computer-based learning it can be undertaken during quiet periods so production and other work is not lost. This can be an area of substantial savings.
- retention – computer-based learning is often retained longer than conventional approaches
- time – the time to achieve the learning outcomes is frequently shorter for computer-based learning.

Summary of key points

General issues

- Formative evaluation can improve the quality of learning materials.
- Summative evaluation can help you judge the success of the development compared to the original objectives.

Methods

- Methods of evaluation include learner feedback, expert reviews, observation, speak aloud, computer logging, tests, questionnaires, interviews and combinations of methods.

Checklists

- Many organizations have made standards for computer-based learning available (for example, Learndirect, Technologies for Training and Institute of IT Training).

Representative samples

- Evaluation is dependent on involving a representative sample of learners.

Cost effectiveness

- Cost effectiveness is a key issue in evaluating computer-based learning.
- Computer-based learning costs more to develop than conventional methods but offers significant benefits which can make it more cost effective.

Index

Analysing Learning Needs

Malcolm Craig

The way we work is changing dramatically: shouldn't the way we analyse training needs be changing too? That question lies at the heart of Dr Craig's thought-provoking book. He examines new working patterns, changes in the relationships between skills, the wholesale shift from motor to cognitive skills and the increasing use of part-time workers. Against this background he sets out a holistic approach to what he calls, significantly, 'learning needs'.

According to Dr Craig, the traditional techniques are no longer adequate. Instead he offers a range of 'investigative' methods designed to identify learning needs and determine what kinds of support would be appropriate. After explaining each method he gives examples and case studies showing how it can be applied. In addition there are numerous self-diagnosis sections to encourage readers to relate the ideas and techniques to their own situation. The result is a book that will enable managers and specialists alike to improve the effectiveness of training in their organization dramatically.

Gower

Gower Handbook of
Management Development

Fourth Edition

Edited by Alan Mumford

Gower Handbook of Management Development brings together a distinguished team of contributors from a variety of backgrounds. Their contributions range over the entire spectrum of management development, covering principles, processes and practice. A constant theme is the need to match management development schemes and activities to the needs of specific organizations and the contributions, though widely differing in their origin, all derive from actual experience and are all concerned with application.

Two key features of the book are the attention paid, firstly, to the relationship between management development and managerial effectiveness, and, secondly, to the way in which our knowledge about how managers learn can be applied. New chapters include one on mentoring and coaching and one on interactive video, while there is an increased emphasis on questions of culture - both national and organizational.

This *Handbook* offers an array of information, stimuli and practical guidance that will appeal powerfully to management development practitioners, consultants, personnel specialists and indeed anyone seriously concerned with improving managerial effectiveness.

Gower

Gower Handbook of Training and Development

Third Edition

Edited by Anthony Landale

It is now crystal clear that, in today's ever-changing world, an organization's very survival depends upon how it supports its people to learn and keep on learning. Of course this new imperative has considerable implications for trainers who are now playing an increasingly critical role in supporting individuals, teams and business management. In this respect today's trainers may need to be more than excellent presenters; they are also likely to require a range of consultancy and coaching skills, to understand the place of technology in supporting learning and be able to align personal development values with business objectives.

This brand new edition of the *Gower Handbook of Training and Development* will be an invaluable aid for today's training professional as they face up to the organizational challenges presented to them. All 38 chapters in this edition are new and many of the contributors, whilst being best-selling authors or established industry figures, are appearing for the first time in this form. Edited by Anthony Landale, this *Handbook* builds on the foundations that previous editions have laid down whilst, at the same time, highlighting many of the very latest advances in the industry.

The *Handbook* is divided into five sections - learning organization, best practice, advanced techniques in training and development, the use of IT in learning, and evaluation issues.

Gower

Guide to In-Company Training Methods

Leslie Rae

Learning at the workplace is usually the cheapest way to train - it is often the best. Leslie Rae's book covers the processes and the skills involved in training without incurring the expense of sending people on external courses. The methods he describes range from 'sitting next to Nellie' through delegation, coaching, mentoring, team development and self-development to one-to-one instruction. He explains in detail the structures and techniques required and provides checklists, formats and guidelines to supplement the text.

Both line managers and professional trainers will profit from a study of this important book by one of the UK's best known training experts.

Gower

Handbook of Technology-Based Training

Edited by Brian Tucker, The Forum for Technology in Training

Technology-based training (TBT) has moved a long way since the early days of computer-based training in the 1960s and 1970s. Today it offers a flexible, cost-effective way of meeting the ever increasing need for people to re-skill.

Handbook of Technology-Based Training provides an accessible guide to the potential benefits and pitfalls of this form of training. It describes the evolution of technology-based training; the various technologies and their uses; the benefits of using such flexible learning; the important issues of how to use the technology; how to implement TBT in an organization and where the future might lie. Brian Tucker also deals with choosing and evaluating generic training and the issues of bespoke training, either produced in-house or outsourced.

The *Handbook* is not highly technical, and deals with the issues in a readily understandable way. It uses examples and detailed case studies to demonstrate how nine leading organizations have managed the various issues and how they have benefited from this approach to training. These include Sun Life, Vauxhall, Lloyds Bank, Argos, British Gas and British Steel.

Structured in two parts, the first provides a complete overview of the subject. The second consists of a directory of over 700 generic TBT courseware titles, indexed by subject, title, medium, and producer. Each entry includes the title of the courseware, its purpose and suitability, a brief description, delivery methods, hardware requirements, price and supplier details.

Gower

How To Be An Online Tutor

Julia Duggleby

Five years ago only a few people would have even heard of the Internet, let alone known what it was, or would have made regular use of it. Yet it is now transforming the way that we find things out, shop, play and communicate with each other. Included in that transformation is the way in which we can learn. Not only does the Internet represent a revolution for the learner, it also represents a sea-change in the way that learning is delivered and supported, and the consequent skills and techniques needed by you - the tutor, trainer, lecturer or teacher.

Julia Duggleby's *How to Be an Online Tutor* has arisen out of her experience as both student and tutor on the South Yorkshire Colleges' Consortium's highly successful LeTTOL (Learning to Teach On-Line) course - http://www.sheffcol.ac.uk/lettol/index.html. Consequently, she shows great empathy for the subject and for the tutors or trainers who need to develop their skills.

The book assumes that you have little in the way of technical expertise, perhaps some experience of the World Wide Web and e-mail, but no more. But it isn't intended as a technical primer, rather as a guide to translating what you already do, in terms of training and facilitating learning, into an online environment, either in the conversion of existing courses or in the creation of new courses.

In the process, it explores the nature, benefits and pitfalls of online learning and the technical skills of sourcing materials, planning, designing and testing courses. Despite, or perhaps because of, the use of technology, the online tutor has a very important human role in engaging, reassuring, welcoming and supporting the course members. The book focuses on how to provide a climate in which people can take responsibility for their own learning; how to guide learners through the course, so that they complete it successfully, and how to be a facilitator for learning, leaving the technology and other learners to deliver the content.

Gower

Techniques of Training

Third Edition

Leslie Rae

There will be a warm welcome for this, the third edition of the standard work by one of the best-known names in training. In it Leslie Rae reviews the main methods currently used in training and development. He describes each one briefly, sets out its advantages and drawbacks and shows - with examples and case studies - where and how to deploy it to best effect.

In this edition the text has been thoroughly revised to reflect recent developments, including Training and Development NVQs and the changing role of the practitioner. There are new chapters on preparing training events and using training aids. The result is a book that will be of immense practical value to anyone concerned with developing people.

Gower